A Quick Review of Statistical Thinking (QRST)

Third Edition

Richard M. Wielkiewicz

College of Saint Benedict/Saint John's University

First Edition: 26 March 2016

Second Edition: 26 April 2017

Third Edition: 26 August 2019

© 2020 Main Event Press

Preface

A Quick Review of Statistical Thinking (*QRST*) is for students who need to quickly become familiar with the content of a typical introductory statistics course as they conduct their own research, begin an honors thesis, take advanced statistics courses, review for the MCAT, or start graduate school. *QRST* covers the main topics in a typical undergraduate statistics course. The only computation covered is the standard deviation. My goal was to condense the typical undergraduate statistics course into a book that could be quickly reviewed. Electronic publishing was chosen to save paper and for cost effectiveness. Each chapter ends with an exercise or quiz, with an answer key, to test your understanding of concepts. Chapter 8 explains how to use IBM SPSS Statistics software (SPSS) to perform statistical analyses covered in the typical undergraduate course and some additional procedures that researchers will find useful, such as recodes, reliability, data transformations, and multiple regression. Examples of reporting the results in articles or papers are also provided.

Instructors of advanced statistics and research methods courses will find that *QRST* can be used as a text in the first week to review or cover basic introductory statistics. *QRST* would also make a good companion text in a course that combines research methods and statistics.

This book has two important help features. First, the detailed table of contents can be used to jump directly to any section of the book. Second, the book includes a glossary. Words defined in the glossary are printed in **bold** the first time they are used in the text.

The third edition of *QRST* was edited extensively. The main changes are to Chapters 3, 6, and 8. These chapters now cover the essentials of confidence intervals and related statistical issues such as meta-analysis.

About the author: Richard M. Wielkiewicz is a Professor of Psychology at the College of Saint Benedict and Saint John's University in central Minnesota. He has been teaching statistics for over forty years. He has published on a wide variety of topics including leadership, evolutionary psychology, effects of study abroad, lifelong learning, the differential outcomes effect, community psychology, behavior management, conservation psychology, perfectionism, intelligence testing, and learned helplessness. He has written eight books including a pair of fiction works on BMX racing.

Reprints of screen shots are Courtesy of International Business Machines Corporation, © International Business Machines Corporation. SPSS Inc. was acquired by IBM in October, 2009. IBM® and SPSS® are registered trademarks of International Business Machines Corporation. IBM, the IBM logo, ibm.com, and SPSS are trademarks or registered trademarks of International Business Machines Corporation, registered in many jurisdictions worldwide. Other product and service names might be trademarks of IBM or other companies. A current list of IBM trademarks is available on the Web at "IBM Copyright and trademark information" at www.ibm.com/legal/copytrade.shtml.

Contents

Chapter 1: Descriptive Statistics

Descriptive statistics visually or numerically summarize a group of numbers. A visual display presents the numbers in a graph or table. A numerical summary is created by calculating a measure of central tendency such as the mode, median, or mean, and/or a measure of variation such as the range or standard deviation. Both numerical and visual summaries assist a researcher in comprehending the meaning of a dataset. They also allow the researcher to assess whether the data resemble a normal or bell-shaped curve which is a prerequisite for most statistical tests.

Displays of Numerical Information

Graphic displays and tables are essential for understanding statistics because they reduce a group of numbers to a compact form that makes it easy to grasp their general characteristics. *QRST* will review three numerical displays: the frequency table, histogram, and boxplot. Researchers can identify potential problems in meeting assumptions of statistical tests by looking at these three displays for each variable.

The Frequency Table

Shown below are the answers of 46 students to the question "How many hours per week do you study statistics?" The raw data can be informative, but a frequency table provides a more useful display of the data. A frequency table consists of two columns of numbers. The first column shows the possible values of a variable and the second column shows how many individuals in the sample obtained that value.

5, 4, 3, 7, 7, 3, 4, 4, 3, 6, 7, 6, 6, 4, 15, 3, 7, 5, 4, 10, 5, 2, 4, 1, 1, 4, 2, 4, 4, 3, 3, 3, 2, 2, 2, 1, 1, 2, 2, 4, 4, 3, 2, 8, 5, 1

Table 1-1 shows a frequency distribution for these raw data copied from IBM® SPSS® output. The first column shows possible values for the variable, in this case hours of study. Students responded to this question with a range of 1 hour to 15 hours of weekly statistics study. The second or "Frequency" column shows how many times each choice appeared in the students' reports. Thus, the table shows that 5 students reported studying 1 hour per week, 8 students reported studying 2 hours, 8 students reported studying 3 hours, 11 students reported studying 4 hours, and so on. The next column, "Percent," shows what percent of the individuals reported each level of study. Thus, 10.9% of the total reported 1 hour of study per week. The next column, "Valid Percent" shows the same percentages except that missing data are excluded from the computations. Because there are no missing data in this dataset, "Percent" and "Valid Percent" are identical. The last column "Cumulative Percent" shows a running total percent. Thus, one could make the following statement about the data: "The table shows that 45.7% of these individuals reported studying statistics three hours per week or less."

The cumulative percent column shows the **percentile rank** of each score. The percentile rank is a very important concept in statistics, especially in the interpretation of tests. The percentile rank is defined as the percentage of scores that fall at or below a score. Thus, if your test score fell at the 90th percentile, it means that 90% of the comparison group obtained scores that were equal to or lower than yours. Percentile ranks are used to communicate the meaning of scores to individuals who have taken a test or their guardians. They also enter into the boxplot, which is discussed later.

Table 1-1. How many hours per week do you study statistics?

Hours		Frequency	Percent	Valid Percent	Cumulative Percent
Valid	1.00	5	10.9	10.9	10.9
	2.00	8	17.4	17.4	28.3
	3.00	8	17.4	17.4	45.7
	4.00	11	23.9	23.9	69.6
	5.00	4	8.7	8.7	78.3
	6.00	3	6.5	6.5	84.8
	7.00	4	8.7	8.7	93.5
	8.00	1	2.2	2.2	95.7
	10.00	1	2.2	2.2	97.8
	15.00	1	2.2	2.2	100.0
	Total	46	100.0	100.0	

Histograms

Another way to display these data is to create a histogram. An example of SPSS output for the same data set is shown below in Figure 1-1. Note that a **figure** contains a graphic representation of numbers whereas a **table** contains actual numbers. Tables and figures are numbered separately in APA style writing and in *QRST*. In this case, the horizontal axis of Figure 1-1 shows possible values on the variable (Hours per week of studying statistics) and the height of each bar indicates the frequency with which each value was chosen. The shape of the distribution is much more obvious when the data are presented as a histogram. Clearly, this dataset is not normally distributed (i.e., bell shaped), but most scores are in the center of the distribution and fewer scores are at each tail. One could also describe this distribution as having a slight **positive skew**. That is, there are a few extreme values at the upper (or positive) end of the distribution. A histogram conveys a significant amount of information about the variable that is almost always useful to the researcher. Creating a histogram for each variable is a good method of identifying variables that are not normally distributed. If a variable is not normally distributed, this could violate a key assumption of most statistical tests. There are many ways to assess violations of assumptions and many ways to address such violations.

If a researcher finds that key variables in their study are not normally distributed, the main way of addressing the problem is to use a **data transformation**. A data transformation consists of performing an arithmetic operation on each score in the distribution such as taking the square root and then doing statistical analyses on the square roots instead of the raw numbers. A square root transformation will have a bigger impact on the more extreme values, so it can potentially correct positive skew. See Chapter 7 for more on this topic and Chapter 8 for instructions on how to perform a data transformation using SPSS.

In my opinion the distribution shown in Figure 1-1 is close enough to a normal distribution that the raw data could be used in analyses without a need to be concerned about violating the assumptions of most statistical tests.

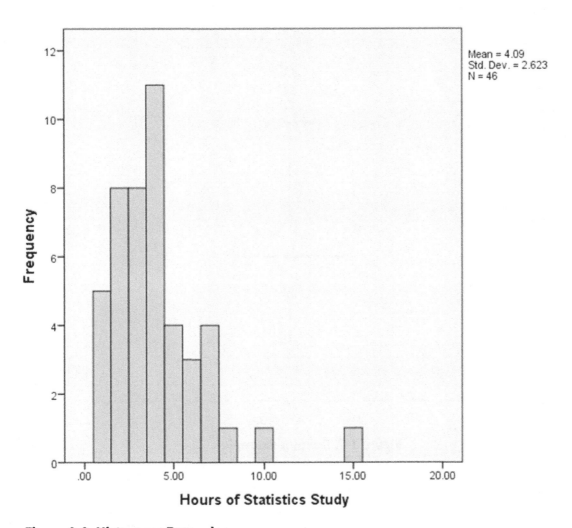

Figure 1-1. Histogram Example

The Boxplot
The boxplot is another way to represent a group of numbers. An important role of boxplots is in identifying **outliers**, individual scores that are outside a reasonable range for the variable being investigated. Outliers deserve additional investigation to determine whether they need to be addressed in some way. One cause of outliers is a typographical error committed while entering the data. For example, an actual grade point average of 3.8 could have been entered as 8.3, which is beyond the typical range for grade point average. This would create an outlier which could easily be corrected. On the other hand, an outlier could represent a person's actual score on a measure, but the score does not accurately represent the person. The person might have responded "strongly agree" to each item of a survey while not paying attention to the content of the items. If this is the case, all the data for this person might need to be deleted. The issue of what to do with outliers or extreme values can be complicated and will be covered in most advanced statistics and research methods courses. However, common sense and honesty in reporting all manipulations of the data should be guiding principles.

A boxplot created by IBM® SPSS® Statistics software (SPSS) is shown in Figure 1-2.

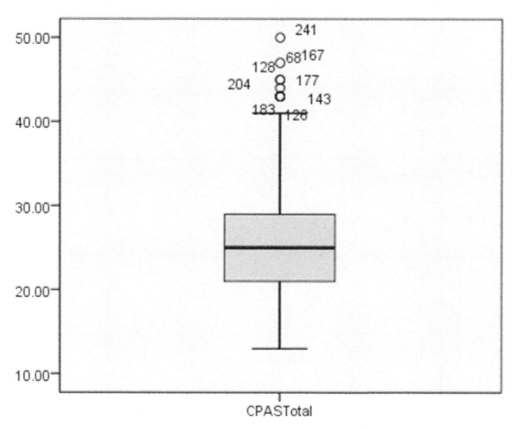

Figure 1-2. Boxplot Example

The variable in Figure 1-2 is CPAS_Total or the total score on the Cell Phone Addiction Scale, a 14-item measure assessing how much a person is dependent upon use of their cell phone and how distressed they become when cell phone use is restricted. Looking at Figure 1-2 it is obvious where the boxplot got its name. The scale on the left shows scores on CPASTotal and the boundaries of the box mark the middle 50% of scores, i.e., from the 25th percentile (CPAS_Total score of about 22) to the 75th percentile (CPAS_Total score of about 28). The dark line in the center is the median (see below for definition). The crossbars at the end of the lines coming out of the box, which look like a capital T and an inverted capital T, are the *whiskers* of the boxplot. Scores beyond the whiskers are defined as outliers and should be the focus of some additional investigation. The numbers associated with each outlier are the row or subject number in the SPSS dataset. When these data were analyzed, outliers were retained in the analysis because they represented people who were truly dependent on their cell phones and distressed when they could not use them. Other strategies for dealing with outliers are to delete them or use a data transformation (see Chapter 7) to reduce their impact.

Descriptive Statistics: Central Tendency

Generally, textbooks divide statistics into two broad areas: **descriptive statistics** and **inferential statistics**. Descriptive statistics are used to describe or summarize characteristics of a group of numbers. It is important to understand descriptive statistics because they are often the only information given in articles appearing in the popular media such as magazines, websites, and blogs.

The other branch of statistics involves making inferences from a sample to a population, thus, the term *inferential statistics*. The focus of any statistics class is upon inferential statistics, but a beginning statistician needs to understand the basic descriptive measures, particularly the mean, because the purpose of many inferential statistical tests is to make inferences about descriptive statistics.

The **mode**, **median**, and **mean** are the three main measures of central tendency that every statistician must know and understand.

Mode

The mode is the most frequent score in a distribution. There is no calculation involved in finding the mode. All you need to do is look at the frequency distribution and find the score with the greatest frequency. That's the mode. Refer to the frequency distribution in Table 1-1 showing hours per week of studying statistics. The largest number of students ($N = 11$) reported studying 4 hours per week so that is the mode. Because this distribution has one clear mode with smaller frequencies as one moves away from the mode, the distribution would be labeled **unimodal**. In a **normal distribution**, the mode, median, and mean are all equal. Consequently, it is desirable in most analyses that a frequency distribution has only one mode.

What about the case where there are two modes? This could be a problem. If the two modes are adjacent this would not be a concern because the distribution could have a relatively normal shape. On the other hand, if there are two modes, separated by an obvious depression, one would be concerned that the data did not conform adequately to a normal shape. An example of a bimodal distribution is shown in Figure 1-3.

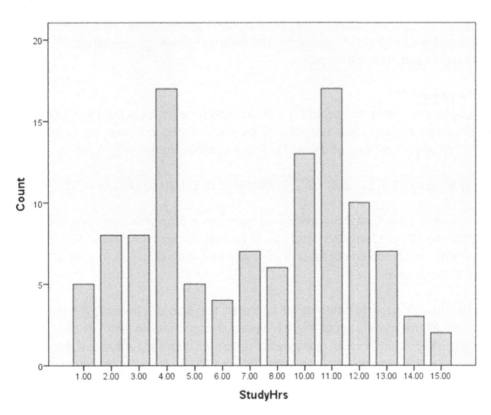

Figure 1-3. Bimodal Distribution

A distribution that looks like this would need further investigation because the shape is clearly not normal, or bell shaped, and it would create problems for typical parametric statistical tests, especially those in the multiple regression family. Furthermore, a distribution would be considered bimodal even when it has two separate modes that are not precisely the same. The fact that the distribution has two clear peaks separated by a valley defines it as bimodal.

Median

The median is the middle score or 50th percentile in a group of numbers. It is not as easy to calculate as you may have been taught in junior high school. The problem is that the median rarely falls exactly on a whole number; instead, it is somewhere inside an interval that contains many scores. Rather than explain exactly how the median is calculated, I suggest letting SPSS do the work. An important characteristic of the median is that it is not affected by the magnitude of extreme scores. For example, if the highest score on a measure was 28 and the median was 10, the high score could be changed from 28 to 528 without affecting the median. The middle score in the distribution would remain 10. Thus, the median is not influenced by outliers. This characteristic of the median sometimes makes it a better indicator of central tendency than the mean.

Mean

The mean or average is by far the most important and most often seen measure of central tendency. It is the sum of all the scores in the distribution divided by the number of scores. Many students learned how to calculate the mean in elementary school. Many of the inferential statistics covered in a typical undergraduate course involve evaluating differences between or among means. The formula for calculating the mean is shown here.

$$M = \frac{\Sigma X}{N}$$

This formula should be instantly recognizable. It says to sum all the values for the variable designated as "X" and then divide the sum by the number of scores in the sample. The mean is influenced by every score in the sample. Thus, if any number in the sample is changed, so is the mean.

The Median versus the Mean

Although the mean is by far the most often reported and analyzed measure of central tendency, its neglected cousin, the median, provides important information about a distribution of scores. Consider, for example, the following scores which represent annual salaries in millions of dollars for a typical professional sport in the US.

.2, .3, .3, .4, .6, .6, .8, 1.0, 1.2, 1.2, 1.3, 1.4, 2.5, 3.6, 5.3, 6.0, 8.0, 10.0, 11.4, 14.6, 32.4, 35.0, 45.0

The median or middle score is 1.3 million dollars whereas the mean is 8.2 million. Which number best represents typical salaries? In this case, the median of 1.3 million dollars most accurately represents the salary of the typical professional athlete, not the mean of 8.0 million dollars because three extreme values (32.4, 35.0, & 45.0) have an inordinate influence and pull the mean upward.

When the mean and the median are very different for a dataset, this provides important information about the data. If the mean and median are approximately equal, there is a good chance that the distribution is roughly normally distributed, which meets a key assumption of many statistical tests. On the other hand, if the mean is substantially higher than the median as in this example, it suggests the distribution is positively skewed, which could be a problem for data analysis. Extreme scores are dragging the mean away from the median. If extreme scores are on the opposite tail of the distribution, it is **negatively skewed**. In sum, the median is an important, but neglected, measure of central tendency that is sometimes the best representative of a "typical score." Combined with the mean, the median can provide an important clue about the shape of the distribution.

Descriptive Statistics: Variation

The concept of variation involves measuring the spread or dispersion of scores around the middle of a distribution. That is, how far away are typical scores from the middle of the distribution? Figure 1-4 shows four hypothetical distributions with increasing amounts of variation: the wider the distribution, the greater the variation. Three measures of variation are covered in this section: the range, the interquartile range, and the standard deviation. By far the most important measure of variation is the standard deviation (*SD*). In fact, it is so important to understand the *SD* that the details of its computation are reviewed in *QRST*. This is the only computation that will be covered.

Range

The range is merely the difference between the highest score and the lowest score. It is not reported much in research articles, but it does have some utility. When calculating the *SD* by hand, it is useful to compute the range because the *SD* is most likely to be around a fifth or sixth of the range and it can never be larger than the range. Using this information, one has a rough cross check on the computations.

Interquartile Range (IQR)
The interquartile range is the distance between scores for the third quartile (Q3) and the first quartile (Q1).
Interquartile range = Q3 - Q1;
- Q1 = 25th percentile
- Q2 = Median (50th percentile)
- Q3 = 75th percentile

The interquartile range is shown by the box in a *boxplot* or *box and whiskers* plot. It is mentioned in *QRST* because of its role in the boxplot.

Variance and Standard Deviation
The variance (SD^2) and standard deviation (SD) are by far the most important measures of variation. Figure 1-4 shows several normal distributions with different amounts of variation. A distribution with no variation at all $(SD^2 = 0; SD = 0)$ would have all scores equal to the same value, i.e., 4, 4, 4, 4, 4, 4, 4. The mean of these values would be 4 $(M = 4)$ and the variation would be zero because the difference between each score and the mean would be zero.

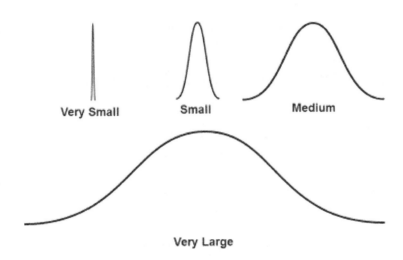

Figure 1-4. Very Small, Small, Medium, and Very Large Amounts of Variation

To find the *SD*, we begin by finding the mean which is the sum of the scores divided by the number of scores. The next step is to compute the variance by subtracting the mean from each score and squaring the difference. Then, find the sum of the squared differences and divide by the number of scores minus one. This value is the variance. The square root of the variance is the standard deviation. Table 1-2 shows how the computation is done.

Computation of the Standard Deviation

Table 1-2. Computation of the Mean, Variance, and Standard Deviation.

Score	Mean	Deviation (X - M)	(Deviation)^2 (X - M)^2
120	181.5	-61.5	3782.25
180	181.5	-1.5	2.25
220	181.5	38.5	1482.25
167	181.5	-14.5	210.25
198	181.5	16.5	272.25
204	181.5	22.5	506.25

Sums

Σ = 1089	--------	Σ = 0.00	Σ (X - M)^2 = 6255.5

$$M = \frac{\sum X}{N} = 1089/6 = 181.5$$

$$SD^2 = \frac{\sum(X-M)^2}{N-1} = 6255.5/5 = 1251.1$$

$$SD = \sqrt{SD^2} = \sqrt{1251.1} = 35.37$$

This is the only computational procedure presented in *QRST* because it is essential to grasp the concept of variation and how the standard deviation works. Hopefully, readers are already familiar with these computations. This example shows computation for a small sample of scores: 120, 180, 220, 167, 198, and 204. To begin, it is necessary to compute the mean of these scores by taking the sum and dividing by the number of scores ($N = 6$). As shown, the mean of the sample is $M = 181.5$. In the next step, the mean is subtracted from each score. The direction of subtraction $(X - M)$ is important because the same subtraction $(X - M)$ is used in the computation of *z*-scores where the sign of the difference has important meaning. When the difference is positive, the score is above the mean and when the difference is negative, the score is below the mean. Thus, to obtain the first deviation score, $X - M = 120 - 181.5 = -61.5$.

Once all the difference scores are obtained it is highly recommended that the sum of these difference scores be computed. It will always be zero, or very close to zero, unless a computational error has been made. Then, all the difference scores are squared which makes them all positive numbers. Finally, adding up the last column provides the sum of the squared deviations, or sum of squares, which is divided by $N - 1$ to equal the variance (SD^2). The square root of the variance equals the standard deviation. Thus, the standard deviation approximates the distance that the typical or average score lies away from the mean of the sample.

A little clarification of the above formula for the variance and standard deviation will be helpful. The formula shown in Table 1-2 for the standard deviation is the *definitional* formula. In other words, it corresponds to the definition of the concept. In some texts and courses, a different version of this formula is seen. This is an algebraically equivalent version that is more convenient for hand computation and computer programming. The two formulas will always produce the same result. However, rounding errors can creep into computations with the definitional formula. To avoid such errors, it is necessary to use enough decimal places. Despite the risk of rounding error, the definitional formula is superior in this context because it provides computational practice consistent with the definition of the concept and encourages a deeper understanding of the meaning of the SD.

An old term for the standard deviation was "root mean square deviation" which sums up the computational procedure but implies that the sum of squared deviations should be divided by N, which would result in a true average, and not $N - 1$. In the computational example shown in Table 1-2 the average squared distance from the mean is obtained by dividing by $N - 1$, instead of N. The reason is that dividing by $N - 1$ gives a more accurate result when the SD of a sample is being used to estimate the SD of the larger population from which the sample was drawn. Inferential statistics computations use $N - 1$ in the denominator, so advanced statistics courses will use $N - 1$ to compute the SD without any explanation. Another name for $N - 1$ is the **degrees of freedom** (*df*). However, some introductory courses will begin presentations on the standard deviation using division by N and transition to $N - 1$ later in the course. After introductory statistics, most computations are done with computer software, not by hand, and the use of $N - 1$ is assumed.

Interpretation of the Mean and Standard Deviation

- Although a mean is often presented by itself, it is preferable to know the mean *and* standard deviation of a variable because the standard deviation can be used to gage whether an individual score is typical or outside the normal range.

- The mean is the most common measure of central tendency. It is influenced by each score in the distribution which is not true for the median and mode. Similarly, the SD and SD^2 are also influenced by each score in the distribution.

- The SD is the *approximate* average distance of scores away from the mean.

- The SD is a quantitative measure of the spread of scores around the mean. The larger the SD, greater the spread or width of the frequency distribution.

- The standard deviation and variance are both measures of variability. The SD is typically the more useful measure compared to the SD^2, because it is in the same units of measurement as the original variable. For example, if you are measuring height, the SD would be in inches whereas the SD^2 would be in units of *square* inches.

- Assuming a normal or near normal distribution, about 68% of scores fall within one standard deviation of the mean. For example, given a distribution with $M = 8$ and $SD = 2.38$, the range of 8 ± 2.38 (5.62 to 10.38) would contain about 68% of the scores.

- The fact that the probability of obtaining a value or range of values can be determined using the mean and standard deviation is at the heart of the process of statistical inference. Probability is the key to separating *noise* (random variation) from *signals* (important changes or statistically significant results).

- One way to view inferential statistics is that the process strictly defines what is meant by *outside the normal range of variation*. That is, we determine the probability of a numerical event and use the probability to evaluate whether the event represents typical random variation or an event that is so unusual that we conclude the result is "statistically significant." Essentially, this process consists of defining the mean and standard deviation of the comparison distribution for the test statistic.

Standardized (z) Scores

The mean and the standard deviation are essential for describing the characteristics of a distribution or sample of scores. However, what if we are interested in the interpretation of just one score in the distribution? A handy metric for this purpose is the z-score. A z-score is defined as

$$Z = \frac{X - M}{SD}$$

The formula says to subtract the mean from the individual score and then divide the result by the standard deviation. The direction of subtraction is critical because the z-score is designed to be a positive number when the raw score (X) is above the mean and a negative number when the raw score is below the mean.

When all the scores for a variable have been converted to z-scores, the variable has been **standardized**. Standardized variables have unique characteristics. First, the mean of z-scores is equal to zero because the mean is zero standard deviations away from the mean. Second, the standard deviation of the standardized variable is equal to one, as is the variance. However, the distribution of z-scores retains the same shape as the original distribution. The question of whether the distribution is "normal" must be pursued separately. In other words, converting a distribution to z-scores *does not* make the distribution normal. Many advanced textbooks discuss standardized scores because assuming a mean of zero and standard deviation of one greatly simplifies presentations of complex statistics.

Z-scores play a crucial role in many applications of statistics. They can be used to find the probability of obtaining a score when the distribution has a normal shape. They can also be used to compare scores from different distributions. For example, imagine a student who has a score of 80 on a test. If the mean and standard deviation of the test are 50 and 10, respectively, the student's z-score is +3.00. In other words, the score is 3.00 standard deviation units above the mean. This is an extremely good score. On the other hand, if the mean and standard deviation of the test are 100 and 15, respectively, the student's score of 80 has a z-score of -1.33. This is well below the mean and does not represent very good performance. Thus, the z-score provides a way to locate an individual score in a distribution, providing its position relative to the mean. It is a very useful way to evaluate scores.

Another important role of z-scores is to provide a way of comparing scores that have different scales, that is, means and standard deviations. For example, imagine that an individual has received a score of 60 on a scale that measures depression. The depression scale has a mean of 50 and standard deviation of 10. The same person also has a score of 139 on an anxiety scale with a mean of 100 and standard deviation of 15. The question is which score indicates the more serious clinical problem? The solution is to compute a z-score for each measure. Using the formula for the z-score, the person's score on the depression scale is equivalent to a z-score of 1.00, whereas the score on the anxiety scale is equal to a z-score of 2.60. Clearly, the more serious clinical problem involves anxiety. Thus, z-scores provide a way of comparing scores from scales with different means and standard deviations.

The Normal Curve and Probability

The z-score can be used to determine the probability of outcomes if certain assumptions are met. Probability is an essential concept in statistics. It is at the heart of the process of statistical inference. We associate a low probability of a statistical result with rejection of the null hypothesis and support for the research hypothesis. In other words, low probability is associated with a successful study. Probability is a complex area of study, but your intuitive understanding of the concept is enough to comprehend inferential statistics. In statistics, probability is presented as a decimal value ranging from 0.0 to 1.00. For example, in statistics, we say $p < .05$ or $p = .003$ if SPSS output is being reported. You must be comfortable with probabilities expressed as decimals because reading and interpreting such probabilities is at the core of statistical inference.

The Normal Curve

The normal curve is defined by a complex mathematical equation. It is an essential concept in statistics because any variable, which is the sum of many random factors, will distribute in the shape of a normal curve. The proof is part of the **Central Limit Theorem**, the most important mathematical proof in statistics. Because so many variables are influenced by many randomly determined factors, the normal curve is ubiquitous in nature. Furthermore, when the raw scores are not normally distributed, the distribution of the means will tend to be closer and closer to a normal curve as the sample size increases. Thus, the Central Limit Theorem assures us that most distributions used in statistical tests are normally shaped. The distributions in Figure 1-4 are all normal curves. The way that we navigate around a normal curve is to calculate z-scores. Furthermore, calculus can be used to determine the percent of the area of a normal curve above or below any z-score. Instead of using calculus, the percentage of areas under the normal curve can be looked up in a table that can be found online or in many statistics textbooks. Two things can be done with the information in a normal curve table.

First, the information can be used to determine the percentile rank of an individual. For example, a Reading Test score ($M = 100$; $SD = 15$) of 120 would have a z-score of 1.33. Using a normal curve table, it can be determined that 90.82% of scores lie at or below this value. This is the percentile rank for a Reading Test score of 120. Percentile ranks are used to clarify the results of most educational and psychological tests. A test interpreter might say "Your Reading Test score was 120. This means that you scored at or above 91% of the people who have taken this test."

Another application of the normal curve table is that it can be used to conduct elementary hypothesis tests to illustrate the process of statistical inference. For example, imagine that a researcher has a reading skill improvement program that they wish to test on one individual. A person is picked to participate in the program and at the end is given a Reading Test. How does the researcher know if the person's reading skill has changed? One way is to set up a hypothesis test that assumes a high score on the Reading Test indicates that the program was successful. Typically, researchers assume that a probability of .05 or less that their result occurred by chance or random variation is enough evidence to reject the null hypothesis and show support for the research hypothesis. However, there's a little twist to this. The .05 probability is divided in half so that the score must be in the upper or lower .025 (or 2.5%) of the distribution. This is called a two-tailed test because both the upper and lower tails of the distribution are included. If the hypothesis test is conducted using z-scores, a value above +1.96 or below -1.96 would be statistically significant. A two-tailed test at the .05 level of significance is the gold standard for published research. *QRST* will not cover one-tailed tests because they have little practical use in research.

To conclude the example, z-scores on the reading test **beyond** either +1.96 or -1.96 would be needed to reject the null hypothesis and support the research hypothesis. That is the equivalent of scores on the Reading Test of 129 or 71. If the individual being studied obtains a score that is beyond either of these scores, a significant change in Reading Test performance is assumed to have occurred. Obviously, a higher score supports the efficacy of the reading improvement program whereas a lower score would require detailed investigation to find out what went wrong.

Most readers of *QRST* have enough background to realize that the preceding example is a terrible study. It lacks a control group; underrepresents any population of interest because there is only one subject; and does not assess the participant's reading performance before the program. In fact, I have never seen a hypothesis test using z-scores in modern research articles. Nevertheless, this is a useful instructional model of how the process of statistical inference works and some version of this kind of hypothesis test appears in many introductory statistics books. Chapter 6 of *QRST* thoroughly reviews the process of statistical inference.

Test your understanding of Chapter 1 by answering the questions that follow. Correct answers are provided after the questions.

Review Questions for Chapter 1

1. What form of numerical display has one column with the possible values of the variable and a second column showing how many of the scores had that value?

2. The percentage of scores that lie below a particular score in a distribution is called _____.

3. Positive skew indicates that extreme values are to the _____ and negative skew means that extreme values are to the _____.

4. Scores that lie beyond the whiskers of a boxplot are called _____.

5. The score that lies at the 50th percentile of a distribution is called _____.

6. Extreme scores in a distribution tend to drag the mean <u>away from / toward</u> [choose one] the median.

7. What are the three main measures of central tendency?

8. Which measure of central tendency is the sum of all the scores divided by the number of scores?

9. Which measure of central tendency is found by subtracting the mean from each score, squaring the difference, finding the sum of the squared differences and dividing the sum by the number of scores minus one?

10. Which measure of variation is in the same units of measurement as the original scores?

11. What percent of scores in a normal distribution lies between one standard deviation below the mean and one standard deviation above the mean?

12. A _____ indicates the number of standard deviation units that a raw score lies above or below the mean.

Answers to Chapter 1 Review Questions

1. frequency table
2. the percentile rank
3. right; left
4. outliers
5. the median
6. away
7. mode median, mean
8. mean
9. variance; the SD is found by taking the square root of this value
10. standard deviation
11. 68%
12. z-score

Chapter 2: Levels of Measurement and Statistical Analysis

Statistics textbooks cover levels of measurement with varying amounts of thoroughness and enthusiasm. The topic earns a chapter in *QRST* because a variable's level of measurement is related to the correct statistical analysis for a research scenario. There are four levels of measurement: nominal, ordinal, interval, and ratio. However, differences among the ordinal, interval, and ratio categories are blurred when deciding upon the appropriate statistical test.

Statistical tests consist of two primary categories: **parametric** and **nonparametric**. Parametric tests make assumptions about the underlying population distributions. Two key assumptions are that populations have normal distributions and population variances are the same (homogeneous) for the groups in the study. In contrast, nonparametric tests do not make such restrictive assumptions. Parametric tests have more statistical power, and, other things being equal, are more likely to produce statistically significant results. Nonparametric tests have less restrictive assumptions, so they are useful when other tests are not. The main purpose of discussing levels of measurement is to guide researchers toward selecting the appropriate parametric or nonparametric statistical test.

The Four Classic Levels of Measurement

Measures can be classified into four categories based upon the type of information that the numbers convey. Most psychological variables measure hypothetical constructs, where the thing being measured is not directly observable. Hypothetical constructs include such things as depression, intelligence, attractiveness, anxiety, motivation, addiction, impulsiveness, etc. Measures of psychological constructs are created in a rational way that leads to a score or measure of the amount of the construct for each individual. However, it is challenging to pin down the precise properties of these measures. Instead of classifying measures as having nominal, ordinal, interval, or ratio properties, researchers construct measures with roughly normal distributions, so they meet the assumptions of the most powerful statistical tests. The classic levels of measurement point toward statistical analysis options for cases where a variable does not meet the assumptions of parametric tests, and help researchers remain aware of the nature of their measures. Descriptions of the four classic levels of measurement and their practical usefulness are below.

Nominal

Nominal measures convey no information about the individual except identifying a category to which they belong or identifying a person. The number does not tell *how much* of any characteristic the individual possesses. One's social security number or a student number assigned by an educational institution are examples of nominal variables. They are another way of coding a person's name that has the advantage of being less ambiguous than common names shared by many people. The numbers on football players are also a nominal label. Another important role of nominal variables is to code variables that indicate group membership such as in a survey or study. An obvious example is coding the variable gender. Statistical programs are designed to use a number rather than a word (called a string variable in SPSS) to designate group membership. Thus, to code gender for statistical analysis, males could be coded as "1," females coded as "2," and prefer not to answer coded as "3." Alternately, an experimental group could be coded as "1," one control group as "2," and another control group as "3." Recognizing nominal variables is critical because they identify group or category membership in research designs.

Nominal variables are typically recognized by the number of levels in the variable and the information communicated by the numeric values of the variable. Typically, the number of levels is relatively small, ranging from two to about five or six. Furthermore, the numeric value communicates group membership, not the amount of a characteristic. Because the numeric values communicate group membership rather than the amount of a characteristic, assignment of numbers to each category is arbitrary. For example, in coding the variable of gender in a study, it is irrelevant as to whether males are coded as zero, one, two, or even three. The value merely communicates group membership and nothing else. However, researchers must keep a record or use SPSS value labels (see Chapter 8) so you don't lose track of the coding scheme.

When a researcher is only interested in the frequency counts for nominal variables, a group of specialized tests (chi-square and others) is used to analyze the frequency counts. Subsequent chapters cover these applications. In sum, nominal variables identify or categorize individuals but do not tell how much of a characteristic that the individual possesses. Nominal variables are grouping variables in some studies and analyzed with specialized tests when frequency counts are the primary focus.

Ordinal

The ordinal level of measurement applies when we know that individuals have more or less of a characteristic than others but we do not know *how much* more or less. A classic example of ordinal measurement is the finish in a race, first, second, or third. We know that first place was faster than second place, but we do not know *how much* faster. The second-place finisher could have been hundredths of a second or minutes behind the first place finisher. Another classic example of an ordinal measure is to have a group line up according to height. If the shortest person is assigned the value of "1," the next tallest person a value of "2," and so on, this would be an ordinal or rank-ordered variable. The numbers assigned to each person indicate that they are taller than those with lower numbers but the exact height of each person or the differences in height from person to person are unknown. It is extremely unusual to transform a variable like height to a rank-ordered or ordinal variable because the transformation from height in feet/inches or centimeters to an ordinal measure would lose so much information about individuals.

In the past, it was argued that psychological constructs such as depression or motivation cannot be precisely measured and that even the best measures could only distinguish whether an individual has more or less of the characteristic than another. For example, if individuals rate their happiness on a numerical scale of 0 to 9, it could be argued that the numbers do not represent the amount of happiness, only that people who respond with higher numbers have reported more happiness than those with lower numbers. Therefore, it was argued that most psychological constructs only had the characteristics of ordinal measures because they did not indicate precisely how much of the measured characteristic the individual possessed. The argument continued by claiming that most psychological variables could be analyzed using only specialized nonparametric tests (e.g., Siegel, 1956). Modern statisticians focus on measures with normal or close to normal frequency distributions, including simple 1 to 9 rating scales. Confirming a variable has a normal distribution, thereby meeting a key assumption of the most powerful parametric statistical procedures, opens the door to a diversity of statistical procedures so the researcher can answer complex questions about their data.

An interesting practical problem is the level of measurement for college class or year which is usually designated as first-year, sophomore, junior, or senior. On the one hand, one could argue that this is an ordinal measure because each level has more of something (education or college credits) than the previous level. On the other hand, most statistical analyses treat college class as a categorical or grouping variable, ignoring its ordinal properties. College class is not a quantitative variable because, with only four levels, a normal distribution is unattainable. Furthermore, mean college class is not a useful descriptive statistic. Instead, it would be more informative to report the number or percent of individuals in each category.

In sum, the minimal characteristic of the ordinal level of measurement is a numerical scale in which higher numbers indicate higher levels of a trait. If the frequency distribution of the variable is shaped like a normal curve, parametric tests are used. If the distribution is not normal, nonparametric tests are used. It is rarely necessary to resort to nonparametric tests.

Interval

Most psychological measures are assumed to be at the interval level of measurement. The interval level of measurement is so-named because the distances between numbers on the scale represent the same amount or quantity of the characteristic being measured. That is, intervals of the measure are theoretically equal. For example, the distance between 2 and 4 on an interval scale is the same amount of the characteristic as the distance between 6 and 8. An interval scale lacks a true zero. In other words, the complete absence of the trait or characteristic is ambiguous. Almost all psychological measures are assumed to have the characteristics of an interval scale. A scale for depression or intelligence provides a fairly precise indication of the amount of intelligence or depression the person has but zero on the scale is undefined. This is accomplished by defining the amount of the characteristic as being related to how far everyone is above or below the mean. However, it may be questionable whether these measures really have equal intervals and researchers do not debate whether a measure has interval properties; they are more concerned whether the variable approximates a normal distribution. Variables with interval properties are analyzed using parametric statistical tests if the distribution approximates a normal curve.

Ratio

A ratio scale has the characteristics of an interval scale plus it has a true and interpretable zero. Height, weight, number of hours of sleep, heartrate, reaction time, and number correct on a test of knowledge are examples of the ratio level of measurement. The name, ratio, comes from the fact that it is possible to say that one individual has twice the amount of the characteristic as another individual when there is a true zero. For example, a person who weighs 200 pounds is twice the weight of a person who weighs 100 pounds. That is, a meaningful ratio of weights can be formed. Not very many psychological measures have ratio properties because they are constructed with the goal of a normal distribution and a true zero is not needed. It was once assumed that the mathematical calculations of most statistics require ratio measures, but this is no longer the case. Instead, parametric statistical analyses require a reasonable approximation of a normal distribution. In sum, measures of most psychological constructs do not approach the ratio level of measurement because a true zero point is irrelevant. The focus is on the distribution of the variable. Variables with the properties of a ratio scale are analyzed with parametric statistics if the distribution approximates a normal curve.

Quantitative and Scale Data

Thousands of written pages have discussed subtle differences among the four levels of measurement. For example, one argument was that division was disallowed as a mathematical operation when the level of measurement was interval because the absence of a true zero meant that forming ratios was illogical. Fortunately, most of these arguments have been resolved in a way that simplifies application of levels of measurement to statistical analysis.

Lord (1953), for example, wrote a hilarious commentary on the statistical treatment of football numbers. Even though football numbers are clearly nominal measures because they only label a player, it can still make sense to compute their averages and compare them. One could ask, for example, whether certain types of players (quarterbacks, running backs, receivers, etc.) have lower numbers than other players (defensive lineman, offensive lineman, etc.). In this case, computing means and comparing them statistically makes perfect sense. The basic point of Lord's thought experiment was that numbers are numbers and they retain their numerical properties no matter where they came from. Thus, strict correspondence between level of measurement and the appropriate statistical test is not needed.

A simplification has been to combine the ordinal, interval, and ratio levels of measurement, and various names are given to this combined category. The term **quantitative** will be used in *QRST*. The result is a system that has three categories: nominal, ordinal and not normally distributed, and quantitative, with this last category having alternate names, such as score and scale (used by the SPSS program). Ordinal measures that are reasonable fits to the assumption of having a normal distribution, are labeled quantitative variables, thus avoiding the debate over whether a measure meets the requirement of equal-intervals. If the variable is not normally distributed, it could be classified as or transformed into an ordinal measure and analyzed using one of the specialized tests for ordinal data. However, the Central Limit Theorem proves that regardless of the shape of the original distribution, a sampling distribution of means will tend toward a normal distribution as sample size increases. Furthermore, a variable that is the sum of randomly determined variables will tend to be normally distributed, anyway. Consequently, nonparametric tests are rarely needed because most psychological measures conform to the requirement of having a normal distribution. Table 2-1 summarizes this approach to classifying variables.

Another option for handling ordinal variables in some cases is to classify them as grouping or nominal variables. For example, consider the variable of college class or year. Its levels are First-year, Sophomore, Junior, and Senior. How should this variable be used in data analysis? Each of the college classes has more or less college credits, or educational experience, than the other levels. Thus, college class might appear to be an ordinal variable. However, most researchers have no interest in computing a measure of central tendency for college class or evaluating whether it might be normally distributed. In sum, its characteristics do not allow it to be classified as a quantitative measure. Instead, for data analysis purposes, college class is a nominal or grouping variable. When a variable has only several categories or levels, it is typically used as a grouping variable in analyses.

Table 2-1. Levels of Measurement and Choosing a Statistical Test

Classic	Generic	Practical
Nominal	Nominal/ Categorical	• Grouping Variable for many tests • Use chi-square & related tests when frequency is the dependent variable.
Ordinal	Ordinal or Quantitative or Scale (SPSS)	• Use nonparametric tests if mean is illogical, or distribution is not normal. • A data transformation might normalize the distribution. • Treat as quantitative and use parametric tests if shape tends toward normal and the mean is a logical descriptive statistic.
Interval	Quantitative or Scale (SPSS)	• Use parametric tests if shape tends toward normal and mean is a logical descriptive statistic.
Ratio	Quantitative or Scale (SPSS)	• Use parametric tests if shape tends toward normal and mean is a logical descriptive statistic.

Let me explain why this approach has emerged using the example of college grade point average or GPA. A student's GPA is the average of the grades they have obtained in the courses they have completed. It is computed by assigning 4 points to a grade of A, 3 points to a B, 2 points to a C, 1 point to a D, and 0 to an F, and then computing the mean of all the grades a student has earned (weighting for number of credits per class). Thus, a student's GPA is a number ranging from 0.00 to 4.00. There are lots of issues with GPA as a measure. There is a ceiling effect because it is impossible to obtain a value above 4.00, leaving a cluster of students at a GPA of 4.00 with no way to differentiate among them. Most colleges require a GPA above 2.00 to graduate or continue registering for courses. This places a restriction on the number of students at the lower levels of GPA. In addition, would it be reasonable to argue that the difference between GPAs of 2.20 and 2.30 is the same as the difference between GPAs of 3.90 and 4.00? In fact, how would one go about constructing an argument and answering this question? Thus, the assumption of equal intervals is doubtful. Despite these measurement issues, researchers classify GPA as a quantitative variable, because the group average of GPAs is an intuitively sound measure and the typical distribution of GPAs has a peak at the center and tapers down beyond the mean. Furthermore, the Central Limit Theorem states that a distribution of means tends toward a normal distribution with increasing sample size, regardless of the shape of the distribution of individual scores. In other words, in the typical study with a reasonable sample size, GPA *means* will be distributed in a roughly normal (bell shaped) curve. Therefore, we treat GPA as a quantitative measure with a normal distribution, which means a variety of sophisticated and powerful parametric statistical procedures can be applied to it. This argument generalizes to a host of other psychological variables that are difficult to classify but are nevertheless treated as quantitative measures.

Another way to approach the problem of deciding whether a variable is quantitative is to consider whether it makes sense to compute a mean. If the number of categories or possible values of the variable is too small, the distribution is clearly bimodal (two peaks), the values cannot be placed in a logical order, or a mean is illogical for other reasons, I suggest that the variable is either categorical or should be treated as an ordinal, not quantitative, variable. For example, Facebook allows a member to choose from a list of 51 gender options. With so many values, it would seem that taking an average would be an option. However, given our limited understanding of gender, it would be impossible to place the values in any logical order in which a higher number meant "more" of something, so a mean would communicate something meaningful. Therefore, it would make most sense to consider this a categorical variable. Thus, the concept of levels of measurement provides guidelines for classifying variables and choosing the appropriate statistical test, but good judgement and common sense are needed, as well.

Quantitative Variables versus Grouping Variables

In the remainder of *QRST*, the two most important categories of measurement are quantitative with an approximately normal distribution (referred to as "quantitative") and categorical, where the numbers are used to indicate group membership. The decision regarding the appropriate statistical analysis hinges on identifying what role these two levels of measurement play in the experimental design. When a variable does not have properties that lead to a roughly normal distribution, the specific statistical tests designed for ordinal measures might be a good fit. This would be a rare event because there are various ways to address these issues that do not rely on nonparametric tests, such as transforming the data. A practice exercise in classifying variables follows with an answer key after the exercise.

Practice in Classifying Variables

One of the most important clues in deciding upon the most appropriate statistical technique is the nature of the variables involved in the study. Variables can be classified as nominal (categorical), ordinal, or quantitative data. The importance of these classifications is that the kinds of variable in the study provide an important clue about the type of data analysis that would be appropriate. For each example, circle the correct level of measurement. An answer key follows the exercise.

1. Biological sex.
   Nominal/categorical   Ordinal with Non-normal distribution   Quantitative

2. ACT or SAT scores.
   Nominal/categorical   Ordinal with Non-normal distribution   Quantitative

3. Height in inches.
   Nominal/categorical   Ordinal with Non-normal distribution   Quantitative

4. A group of ten people is assigned a number that represents their relative height in the group with a "1" indicating the tallest person and a "10" assigned to the shortest person. The distribution is not normal.
   Nominal/categorical   Ordinal with Non-normal distribution   Quantitative

5. Social security number.
   Nominal/categorical   Ordinal with Non-normal distribution   Quantitative

6. Year in college (i.e., first-year, sophomore, junior, senior).
   Nominal/categorical   Ordinal with Non-normal distribution   Quantitative

7. Answers to this True/False question: I am afraid of the dark.
   Nominal/categorical   Ordinal   Quantitative

8. Students involved in (1) no organized sport, (2) an intramural team, (3) a varsity athletic team. Nominal/categorical Ordinal with Non-normal distribution   Quantitative

9. A depression scale with scores ranging from 5 to 25 and roughly normally distributed.
   Nominal/categorical   Ordinal   Quantitative

10. A question asking students to report whether their high school was small, medium, or large.
    Nominal/categorical   Ordinal with Non-normal distribution   Quantitative

11. Scores on an intelligence test.
    Nominal/categorical   Ordinal with Non-normal distribution   Quantitative

12. Students are asked the following question: Do you have a significant other at the present time? YES   NO
    Nominal/categorical   Ordinal with Non-normal distribution   Quantitative

13. Students are asked to rate their current level of happiness on a scale ranging from 1 to 9.
    Nominal/categorical   Ordinal with Non-normal distribution   Quantitative

14. Students are asked to rate themselves on the following scale: (1) Happy, (2) Neutral, (3) Sad.
    Nominal/categorical   Ordinal with Non-normal distribution   Quantitative

15. Order of finish in a race.
    Nominal/categorical   Ordinal with Non-normal distribution   Quantitative

16. The number of miles per gallon for each vehicle in a group.
    Nominal/categorical   Ordinal with Non-normal distribution   Quantitative

17. Scores on a quiz where scores can range from 0 to 100.
    Nominal/categorical   Ordinal with Non-normal distribution   Quantitative

18. Answers to a question with these options: (1) male, (2) female.
    Nominal/categorical   Ordinal with Non-normal distribution   Quantitative

19. A research study participant is shown fives pictures and asked to order them from most to least masculine.
    Nominal/categorical   Ordinal with Non-normal distribution   Quantitative

20. A research study places participants in one of three groups. What is the level of measurement for "group membership?"
    Nominal/categorical   Ordinal with Non-normal distribution   Quantitative

Answers are on the next page.

Answers to Exercise

1. Nominal/categorical
2. Quantitative
3. Quantitative
4. Ordinal
5. Nominal/categorical
6. Nominal/categorical [The most practical approach is to call this a categorical variable because it could be used to determine group differences for other variables.]
7. Nominal/categorical
8. Nominal/categorical
9. Quantitative
10. Nominal/categorical
11. Quantitative
12. Nominal/categorical
13. Quantitative [Endless pages could be devoted to debating this answer. However, when the variable contains this many levels it makes sense to analyze it as a quantitative variable. Others may disagree.]
14. Nominal/categorical
15. Ordinal
16. Quantitative
17. Quantitative
18. Nominal/categorical
19. Ordinal
20. Nominal/categorical

Chapter 3: The Pearson Correlation Coefficient

A Pearson correlation coefficient provides a measure of the degree of *linear* relationship between two *quantitative* variables. For example, if a researcher wishes to determine whether a relationship exists between students' GPAs and number of hours they study per week, a correlation coefficient would be the appropriate analysis. Generally, one would expect higher GPAs to be associated with more study hours per week, but the relationship would be far from perfect. Instead, one might expect a general trend of more study hours being associated with higher GPAs. The correlation coefficient provides a measure of the strength of the relationship. Correlation plays such a key role in data analysis that it has its own chapter in *QRST*.

The Scatterplot

A scatterplot is a visual representation of the relationship between two *quantitative* variables. The process of making a scatterplot is almost the same as plotting a simple linear graph. In a scatterplot, the relationship is not perfectly linear. Instead, the points can fall anywhere on the graph. The closer the points on the graph come to clustering around a straight line, the stronger the correlation between the two variables. Several scatterplots will be used to illustrate points about the correlation coefficient in this chapter. Constructing a scatterplot begins with two pieces of quantitative information about everyone under study. For example, a survey could ask students for their current cumulative GPA and the number of hours they study per week. Then a graph is constructed with possible GPA values on one axis and possible values for study hours on the other axis. For each person in the study, the intersection of GPA and weekly study hours is found, and a point is plotted at this intersection. For large samples, a scatterplot is easily created with SPSS. A picture of the relationship between GPA and study hours emerges from this process as in the following example. Table 3-1 shows several individuals from a hypothetical study of Study Hours and GPA.

Table 3-1. Hypothetical Relationship between Study Hours and College GPA		
Subject Number	Weekly Study Hours	College GPA
1	15.0	3.44
2	10.0	3.10
3	8.6	2.88
4	5.6	3.00
5	22.0	3.60
6	3.0	1.10
7	7.0	1.00
8	20	1.50
9	15	2.50

The data in Table 3-1 were used to create the scatterplot shown in Figure 3-1. Note that each point on the scatterplot has two numbers directly above it. The first number is Weekly Hours of Study and the second number is GPA. To plot the first point on the lower left of the scatterplot, draw an imaginary vertical line from 3.0 Weekly Study Hours up to an imaginary horizontal line that extends from the GPA scale at 1.1. The intersection of the horizontal and vertical lines is where a point on the scatterplot belongs. This process continues until all the points are plotted. The Pearson correlation between these two variables was $r = .410$, which is between a medium and large effect size. Due to a small sample size ($N = 9$) the result was not statistically significant.

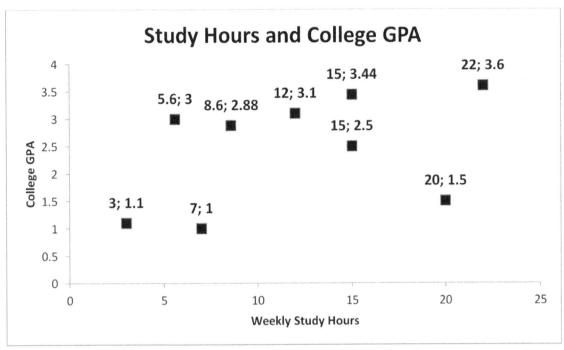

Figure 3-1. Hypothetical Scatterplot of Study Hours and College GPA, *r* = .410

Several more examples of scatterplots are below.

Computation

The correlation coefficient is the average of the cross-products of *z*-scores of the two variables. With a small number of people in the sample, it is easy to compute the correlation between two variables but at sample sizes that make the correlation coefficient a meaningful measure, hand computation is impractical.

Formula for the correlation coefficient:

$$r = \frac{\sum Z_X Z_Y}{N}$$

Computation of the correlation begins with having two measures from each person in the study. For example, one might survey a group of undergraduate students and ask for their college GPAs and the number of hours that they study in a typical week. Computation of the correlation between GPA and Study-hours begins by computing the mean and standard deviation of each variable. The next step is to compute a *z*-score for each value of GPA and each value of Study-hours. Then, multiply each pair of *z*-scores from the same person, take the sum of these cross-products, and divide by the number of pairs of scores. The result is the correlation coefficient.

Characteristics

The range of the correlation coefficient is -1.00 to 0.0 to +1.00. If you happen to be computing the correlation by hand and obtain a value outside this range, you have made a COMPUTATIONAL ERROR. There is no other possibility. Complete absence of a linear relationship results in a correlation of 0.0.

When the correlation is *r* = +1.00, it is a perfect positive correlation and all scatterplot points will land on a straight line with a positive (upward) slope as shown in Figure 3-1.

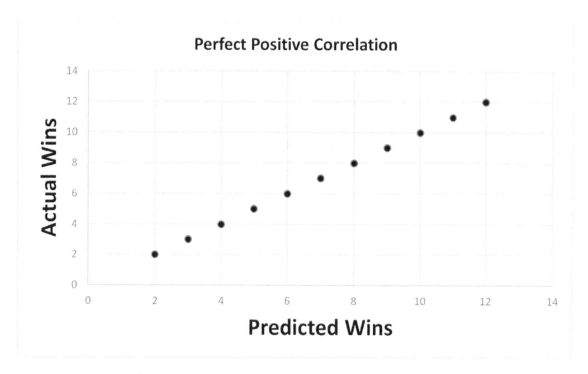

Figure 3-2 Example of a Perfect Positive Correlation

The scatterplot in Figure 3-2 shows hypothetical data for a sports blogger who is predicting the number of wins for each team in a professional league. For this example, each subject is a team with two pieces of information: predicted wins and actual wins. The horizontal axis shows the number of predicted wins for each team. Each dot represents the intersection of predicted and actual wins. Had the blogger correctly predicted the number of wins for each team, the scatterplot would look like the one shown above, and the correlation would be +1.00. Incidentally, when the correlation is +1.00, each pair of z-scores from the same person or pair will be identical.

On the other hand, if the blogger had been completely wrong and each team lost as many games as the blogger predicted it would win, the correlation would be -1.00 as shown in Figure 3-3. All scatterplot points will land on a straight line with a negative (downward) slope. When the correlation is -1.00, each pair of z-scores from the same person or pair will have the same magnitude but the signs will be opposite.

Perfect correlations are somewhat rare and usually trivial in meaning when they are found.

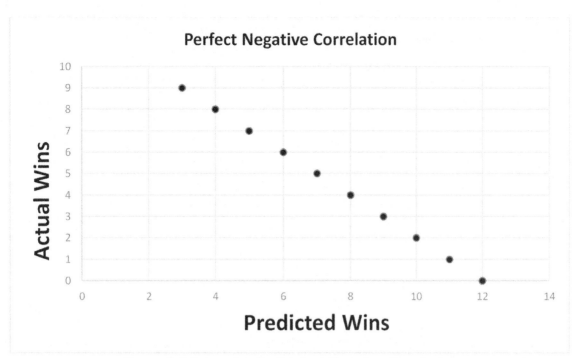

Figure 3-3 Example of a Perfect Negative Correlation

Positive and negative correlations with the same magnitude (e.g., +.76 vs. -.76; +.33 vs. -.33) show the same STRENGTH of relationship. Only the DIRECTION of the relationship is different.

Following are some examples of scatterplots and correlations that illustrate more properties of the correlation coefficient. The correlation coefficient is a measure of the degree of *linear* relationship between two variables. If there is a strong *nonlinear* relationship, the correlation coefficient (r) will not accurately measure the strength of the relationship. Figure 3-3 illustrates this point.

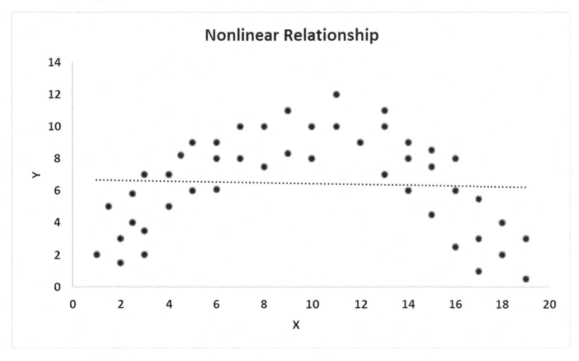

Figure 3-4. Nonlinear Relationship

SPSS was used to compute the correlation for the data shown in Figure 3-4 and the results are shown below in Table 3-2.

Table 3-2. Correlation of Data Shown in Figure 3-3

		X-Values	Y-Values
X-Values	Pearson Correlation	1	-.045
	Sig. (2-tailed)		.764
	N	47	47
Y-Values	Pearson Correlation	-.045	1
	Sig. (2-tailed)	.764	
	N	47	47

Even though there is a very strong *nonlinear* relationship between X and Y, the correlation coefficient is -.045 (and the results fall short of statistical significance by a large margin) as shown by the SPSS output. The reason for this outcome is that the correlation coefficient measures only the degree of *linear* relationship between the two variables. Thus, when a straight line is fit to these data, most of the scatterplot points are away from the line resulting in a correlation coefficient close to zero. If this relationship had been part of a larger study, it is possible that the strength of the relationship would be overlooked because of the low correlation coefficient. It is important that researchers look at the scatterplot for each correlation in their dataset so problems like this can be detected and addressed.

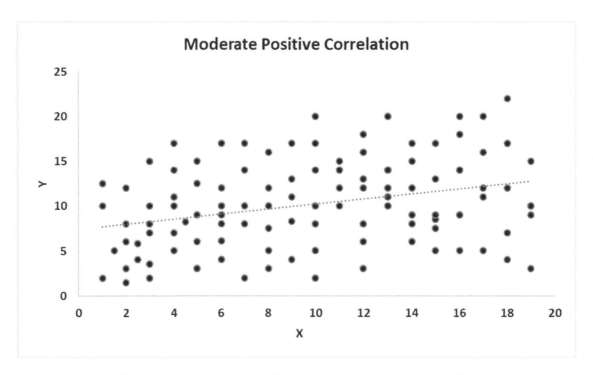

Figure 3-5. Example of a Moderate Positive Relationship

Table 3-3. Moderate Positive Correlation

		X-Values	Y-Values
X-Values	Pearson Correlation	1	.306**
	Sig. (2-tailed)		.001
	N	111	111
Y-Values	Pearson Correlation	.306**	1
	Sig. (2-tailed)	.001	
	N	111	111

**. Correlation is significant at the 0.01 level (2-tailed).

A moderate positive correlation, typical of research results, is shown in Figure 3-5 and the SPSS output in Table 3-3. Note that there is a general trend in the positive direction; as the X variable increases, the Y variable also increases. This is the pattern seen in positive correlations. For a negative correlation, the trend line would slope downward and an increase in X would be associated with a decrease in Y. See Chapter 8 for instructions on using SPSS to compute and interpret correlations.

Restriction of Range

Imagine that the X values in Figure 3-4 had been restricted to a range of 0-6. The resulting correlation would be less due to **restriction of range**. In general, when the range of one of the variables in a correlation is restricted, the correlation is lower, and thus underestimates the true relationship between the two variables. This could happen in any study in which the range of one of the variables is restricted for any reason. As much as possible, studies analyzed with the correlation coefficient should have a sample that represents the entire range of diversity on both variables.

Causality and Correlation

There is a well-known rule that a **causal claim** cannot be made using an association between one variable and another. Another way to say this is "you can't use correlation to infer causation." This is correct, but the rule must be followed using common sense and critical thinking. If you are looking at *one study* involving the correlation between two variables, it is not reasonable to claim that one variable *causes* change in the other. A correlation study lacks characteristics that allow other causes of the relationship to be ruled out. However, there are situations, such as studying the relationship between smoking and lung cancer, where it would be impossible to design a definitive study to prove a causal link because it is not ethical to randomly assign people to be smokers and nonsmokers, a design that would allow a causal claim to be made. Even though evidence of the relationship between smoking and health in humans is based upon correlational research, the accumulated evidence is so massive and overwhelming that it supports the conclusion that smoking *causes* lung cancer and other health problems. As Morling (2015) describes this issue, the most **parsimonious** explanation of the *pattern* of the evidence is that a causal relationship exists. Although the basic caution against using a *single* correlational study to infer a causal relationship holds true, the issue of inferring causation becomes more complex when dealing with difficult real-world problems for which many research findings exist.

Multiple Correlation/Regression

Many people reading *QRST* will be preparing for a course in multiple regression, which is one of the most versatile of all statistical techniques. In contrast to bivariate correlation which involves only two variables, multiple correlation involves using several independent variables in combination to predict a single dependent variable. There are two types of multiple regression: stepwise and hierarchical. Hierarchical multiple regression allows assessment of the relationship between two variables while controlling for another variable. Thus, this technique can be used to examine complex relationships and strengthen causal claims based upon correlations. These two techniques will be briefly defined in the sections on choosing the correct test. Chapter 8 has an example of using SPSS to compute a hierarchical regression. The procedure is incredibly versatile, and you are very likely to learn about it in advanced data analysis courses.

The Squared Correlation Coefficient (r^2)

Squaring a correlation coefficient results in a measure with very interesting properties. Starting with a little background, imagine that you are predicting the value of a variable with no other information. For example, you want to predict the GPA of a college student you have not met. What is the best prediction that you could make? The best you could do is predict that the person has an average GPA. This applies whenever you are predicting the outcome of a quantitative variable. The best prediction is that any individual will be average. Why? Because most quantitative variables have normal or near-normal distributions with most individuals being close to the mean and fewer individuals found further and further way from the mean. Thus, the best bet is to predict the mean when you have no other information on which to base a prediction. From this perspective, the variance (SD^2) of GPA represents the inaccuracy or error that results when the mean is used to predict a value for a person with no additional information about them. Similarly, looking ahead to Chapter 4 on prediction, it is easy to demonstrate that any prediction made when the correlation is zero will result in a predicted value equal to the mean of the dependent variable.

When we have knowledge of another variable that is correlated with the variable we are trying to predict, the situation improves. We can now make a better prediction. For example, if a student's ACT score is known, it would be possible to make a better prediction of their GPA compared to predicting the mean. A measure of the amount of improvement is provided by the squared correlation coefficient (r^2). Alternate terms for the squared correlation coefficient are the "coefficient of determination," "variance accounted for," "common variance," and "shared variance." Another way to conceptualize the squared correlation coefficient is that it tells the researcher how much better the prediction becomes when the correlation is used to make the prediction instead of the mean of the dependent variable. For example, if the correlation was equal to .316, the squared correlation would be .10. Then the researcher might say the independent variable accounts for 10% of the variance or that the two variables have 10% of their variance in common. Alternately, one could say there is a 10% improvement in the ability to predict GPA compared to using the mean. This concept appears in several measures of effect size (see Chapter 6) and computations related to making predictions.

Confidence Intervals and Variability of the Correlation Coefficient

Computation of a single correlation between two variables does not mean that one has found THE correlation between them. If you took another sample from the same population, you are unlikely to obtain the same correlation. Instead, you would expect differences among the computed correlations. Imagine a population in which the correlation between variables X and Y was .30. If numerous samples were taken from this population and the correlation between X and Y (r_{xy}) for each sample was computed, they would not all equal the population value of .30. Instead, the correlations would vary around an average value of .30. Similarly, when a sample value of r is computed, statisticians are interested in finding what the population value might be, given the sample value for r. The **confidence interval** (CI) provides a range of correlations within which the population value is likely to fall. When confidence limits (the endpoints of the confidence interval) are computed, a range of values within which the population value is likely to lie, has been defined. An alternative perspective is to assume that the obtained sample value of r is the best estimate of the population value of the correlation. Then, we see the confidence interval as a range within which future sample values for the correlation are likely to fall. Unlike most confidence intervals, which are symmetrical, the confidence interval around a sample correlation coefficient is asymmetrical. The only time the correlation coefficient has a symmetrical confidence interval is when the value is 0.00, which is not a very interesting case. The reason that non-zero correlation coefficients have asymmetrical confidence intervals is that positive correlations have a ceiling (+1.00) and negative correlations have a floor (-1.00).

Hayes (1988, pp. 592-593) describes computation of a confidence interval for a correlation coefficient. The procedure involves transforming the correlation coefficient, r, into a variable that is roughly normally distributed using Fisher's r to Z transformation. Using the r to Z conversion, upper and lower confidence limits can be calculated using the formulas provided by Hayes. Alternately, one can search the Internet for sites that do the computations for you such as this site. Using both the method described by Hayes and the CI Calculator linked previously, I found that the 95% confidence interval for the sample correlation presented in the previous example (r = .306, N = 111) is .127 - .466. This indicates that the population value has a 95% chance of being found between correlations of .127 and .466. Thus, to be fair and accurately represent the amount of variability surrounding a sample value of r, it is informative to report both the sample value of the correlation coefficient and a confidence interval representing the range within which the population value is likely to be found. Using APA style, one might say the correlation between X and Y was .306, 95% CI [.127, .466]. Thus, if the study were done again with a new sample, and the outcome was a correlation of $r = .135$, the value, though lower, is not out of line with the confidence interval for a correlation of $r = .306$, the original finding. However, the confidence interval for the new correlation, 95% CI [-.053, .313] has now shifted lower and includes the possibility that the correlation comes from a population with a zero correlation. Now what!

Note that the confidence interval for $r = .135$, 95% CI [-.053, .313] includes the original sample value of .306 which is consistent with the original findings. However, the new value of .135 opens the possibility that the population value is zero. Thus, examining confidence intervals shows that a lot of instability is inherent in the computation of a single correlation coefficient. Researchers, therefore, need to be aware of this instability or variability and not overinterpret the results of a single study involving a correlation or any other sample statistic. Due to the inherent variability of all statistical findings, things could change quickly when the study is replicated. Cumming (2014) refers to this phenomenon as the "dance" of the confidence intervals.

How do we bring some order to these dancing confidence intervals? The answer is **meta-analysis**. Meta-analysis is a statistical technique for combining results of many studies. A meta-analysis would take all the studies about a research question, including those that are unpublished or obtained negative results, and combine them into a single estimate or range of estimates of the magnitude of the relationship. In other words, all the relevant results are brought together to bring some order to the range of results. The technique is so critical to the advancement of science, that modern studies considered for publication must include the information needed for inclusion in future meta-analyses. A meta-analysis also examines the coefficients obtained in the studies and investigates whether the magnitude of correlations might be related to characteristics of the studies in which they were obtained. For example, a meta-analysis might find that the correlation of two variables is higher for samples of college students than it is for samples of working adults.

A very important characteristic of confidence intervals (of all kinds, not just r) is that they become narrower as the sample size increases. One way to look at this is to note that the larger the sample size, the more of the population is represented by the sample. Thus, with a larger sample size, the sample value of the correlation is more likely to accurately represent the population value. Consequently, the range of values for the CI is smaller. So, if you want to have a narrow confidence interval, use a larger sample size. The larger sample size will also cause your study to be given more weight in meta-analyses.

Another important lesson from confidence intervals is that they keep researchers aware that the values they find are not written in stone. Variability from study to study, replication to replication, is an inherent part of research. To put this concretely, if you obtain a correlation of .306 in one study, the next time you or someone else calculates this correlation with a different sample, the obtained value for r is very likely to be different. The 95% CI is reported to keep researchers aware of this fact and to allow others to assess the precision of the results, as indicated by the width of the confidence intervals. Narrower CIs indicate greater precision.

A ubiquitous concept in statistics is "statistical significance." That's why almost all statistical computations are accompanied by a statement of probability. In Table 3.3 the correlation of .306 has a probability, Sig. (2-tailed), of .001 associated with it. This probability indicates the likelihood that the correlation of .306 came from a population with a correlation of zero. Because the probability that the correlation of .306 came from a population with a correlation of zero is so low, we reject that idea, and conclude the result is "statistically significant." The logic of making this decision is called NHST, Null Hypothesis Significance Testing, and is reviewed in Chapter 6. Another approach, which leads to the same conclusion is to use confidence intervals to decide about statistical significance. In the case of the correlation coefficient, we look at the 95% confidence interval and ask whether a value of zero falls within the limits. If a correlation of zero is outside the limits of the 95% confidence interval, it is also concluded that there is less than a 5% chance (100% - 95% = 5%) that the sample correlation comes from a population with a zero correlation. Thus, we conclude that the sample comes from a population with a non-zero correlation. In other words, the relationship shown by the sample correlation coefficient is likely to exist in the population. Both looking at confidence intervals and using the logic of NHST lead to the same conclusion. Therefore, it makes sense to ask whether there is any reason to prefer one approach over the other.

This question has been argued fervently by those who prefer one approach over the other, but most researchers employ the NHST approach which was endorsed by Wilkinson and the Task Force on Statistical Inference (1999). On the other hand, authors such as Cumming (2014) argue in favor of completely abandoning NHST in favor of estimation based upon confidence intervals and effect sizes. Cumming says that NHST is "severely flawed," the role of probability in NHST is misunderstood by many researchers who use it, and that estimating confidence intervals is a more intuitive approach. My position is that both NHST and confidence intervals need to be understood by every researcher. However, because NHST dominates the presentation of results in most professional research journals, researchers need to have a full understanding of it. On the other hand, confidence intervals emphasize the variability inherent in all statistical data and provide an intuitive route toward comprehending the meaning of results. Thus, *QRST* will keep a primary focus on NHST while addressing the value added by considering confidence intervals and related concepts such as meta-analysis.

Review Questions for Chapter 3

1. A _____ is a measure of the degree of *linear* relationship between two *quantitative* variables. []

2. When there is no linear relationship between two quantitative variables, the correlation will equal _____.
   []

3. Which of the following correlations represents the strongest relationship? .28; -.76; 0.0; .53

4. Create a scatterplot of the following pairs of scores:

X	Y
10	16
9	10
12	17
5	8
7	7
7	13
4	8
13	19
10	15
11	13
8	12

5. Does the scatterplot shown in Question 4 show a linear relationship? YES   NO

6. Is the relationship shown in Question 4 positive or negative?

7. Which of the following is most likely the computed value of the correlation shown in Question 4? 1.00; .95; .87; .50; .33; 0.0; -.29; -.55; -.67; -1.00

8. The general rule is that you   CAN   CANNOT (choose one) infer causation from a single correlation study.

9. If you are computing a correlation coefficient by hand and find a value of 1.56, what is the explanation?

10. If the scatterplot shows a strong nonlinear relationship, the correlation coefficient is likely to overestimate / underestimate (choose one) the strength of the relationship.

11. The squared correlation coefficient, r^2, is a measure of _____.

12. Imagine that a researcher obtained a correlation of .435 between two variables, X and Y. Use this site to calculate the 95% (.95) confidence limits for this correlation. For one calculation, assume a sample size of 10 (N = 10) and for the second assume a sample size of 500 (N = 500). What confidence intervals were obtained for each sample size? What do the results tell you about the relationship between confidence intervals and sample size? Which of the two results indicate a "statistically significant" result? Why?

Answers to Chapter 3 Questions

1. correlation coefficient
2. zero
3. -.76
4.

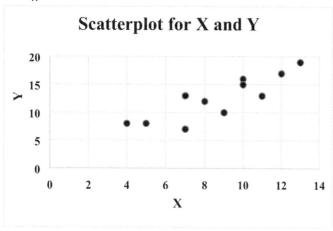

5. YES
6. Positive
7. .87
8. CANNOT
9. You have made a computational error.
10. underestimate
11. How much better a prediction becomes when the correlation is used to make the prediction instead of the mean of the dependent variable. Alternate names for the squared correlation coefficient are the coefficient of determination, "variance accounted for," "common variance," and "shared variance."
12. Given a sample correlation of .435, and a sample size of 10, the 95% CI is [-.268, .836]. When the sample size is increased to $N = 500$, the 95% CI is [.361, .503]. These results show that increasing the sample size causes the confidence interval to be narrower. The confidence interval for the sample size of 10 [-.268, .836] includes a population value of zero. With a sample size of $N = 10$, the obtained sample correlation of .435 could have come from a population for which the correlation was zero. Therefore, it is not statistically significant. On the other hand, when the sample size is increased to $N = 500$, the 95% CI [.361, .503] does NOT include zero so the likelihood that the obtained correlation comes from a population with a zero correlation is very low. Therefore, the idea that the population correlation could be zero is rejected and the results are statistically significant.

Chapter 4: Prediction

Traditionally, introductory statistics textbooks cover prediction in the same chapter as bivariate correlation. The skill involved in prediction is to use the correlation between two variables to predict the score of a person on one variable given their score on the other variable. This is a person who was not in the original study; instead it is a person for whom the score on only one of the two variables is known. For example, many individuals took either the ACT or SAT as a college admission test. Typically, the correlation between the SAT or ACT is used to predict the person's GPA for the first year of college. Because students who take the ACT or SAT have not been to college yet, the ACT or SAT is used to predict their success using the correlation computed from an earlier study. Making such a prediction for *each* applicant is not practical. Instead, the decision on whether to admit each student is typically based upon cutoff scores and other criteria. Thus, the skill of making individual predictions is not useful in most settings.

On the other hand, working knowledge of how to make such individual predictions can be valuable for understanding important issues in measurement, interpreting test scores, and comprehending the concept of reliability. If you are reading *QRST* to prepare for a course in psychological testing or measurement, it may be very helpful to review this chapter. On the other hand, if you are preparing for a course in research methods or advanced statistics, the concepts reviewed in this chapter may not be as important.

Methods of doing Prediction

Three methods of bivariate prediction will be described.
- Read predicted values from the best-fitting straight line
- Use a raw score regression equation.
- Use the standardized regression equation

Read Predicted Values from the Best-fitting Straight Line

This method is approximate and relies on the accuracy of the scatterplot. It would not be used in formal work, but nicely illustrates the principles underlying each of the other methods. To use this method, take the original data and create a scatterplot which includes the best-fitting straight line or regression line. An example is shown below in Figure 4-1. For this example, using hypothetical data, it is assumed that an admissions test is being used to predict first-year students' GPAs. The initial study is done with students who have taken the admissions test and completed their first year of college. A scatterplot has been created with a best-fitting straight line. Reading predicted values from the best-fitting line is easy. Let's assume that an admissions staff member is interested in predicting the GPA of a high school senior who obtained a score of 12 on the Admission Test. To predict this student's GPA, follow a vertical line from the score of 12 up to the best-fitting line. Then, make a 90-degree turn toward the other axis and continue until the GPA axis is intersected. The person's predicted GPA is about 2.4. The dashed red lines in Figure 4-1 show how this is done. The accuracy of this technique depends upon the accuracy and precision of the scatterplot and regression line. Although it is used to illustrate the process, it is not practical or very precise to depend upon an estimate of the predicted score from the scatterplot. A more accurate technique is to use the linear equation for the best-fitting line to make the prediction.

No matter how precise the technique for obtaining the predicted score, the predicted value is an estimate surrounded by variability. The scatterplot itself shows that most points are not on the best-fitting line; so, the score on the independent variable only estimates a range of scores on the dependent variable. There is error associated with the prediction called the **standard error of estimate**. Using the standard error of estimate, it is possible to compute a range of values within which the person's actual score is expected to fall, given the predicted value. Prediction is not perfect. The predicted value is the center of a range of values within which the actual value of the dependent variable for that person is likely to be found.

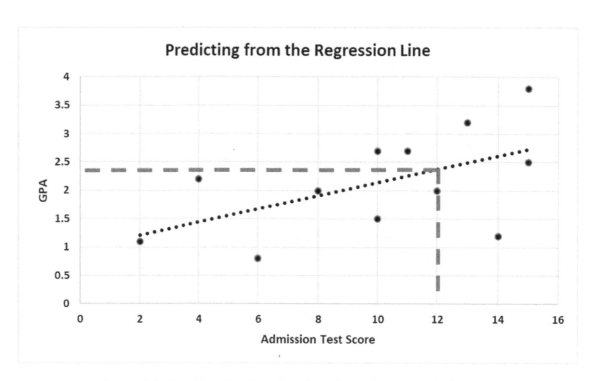

Figure 4-1. Reading Predicted Values from the Best-Fitting Line

Using the Raw Score Regression Equation for Making Predictions

Some texts refer to this as the raw score prediction formula. It is the same technique described above except that the equation of the best-fitting line is used to make predictions. Using the means, standard deviations, and correlation of the two variables, the slope and Y-intercept of the best-fitting line can be computed. This information can then be used to create a linear equation describing the best-fitting straight line. However, most would use SPSS or another program to find the regression equation. SPSS produced the following regression equation for the above dataset:

$$GPA = .117 \text{ (AdminTest)} + .972$$

The equation reads that the predicted GPA equals .117 times the Admission Test Score plus .972.

Substituting a value of 12 for AdminTest results in this solution

$$GPA = .117 \text{ (12)} + .972 = 2.376$$

Thus, this method of finding the predicted value for GPA gives a result of 2.376 which is very close to the estimated value of 2.4, obtained using the previous method. Note that the main feature of this method is that the input is the raw score on the Admissions Test and the output of the equation is the raw score of GPA. As noted in the previous section, the predicted GPA is the center of a range of values within which the actual score is expected to fall.

Prediction Using the Standardized Regression Equation

In my view, this is the most interesting method of making predictions. It is slightly more complex than using the raw score regression equation, but it is easy to remember and illustrates a couple of key principles of regression analysis. In contrast to the above, the standardized regression equation uses z-scores, not the raw scores as the input and output of the equation. The basic form of the standardized regression equation is:

$$Z_Y = \beta \, Z_X$$

This is read as follows: The predicted z-score for Y equals beta times the z-score for X. Beta (β) has a complex meaning in *multiple* regression, but in the *bivariate* (two variables) case, beta is equal to the correlation coefficient. Thus, to use this equation, begin by converting the raw score of X (Admission Test, in this example) to a z-score. Then, enter this z-score into the equation. The output is the z-score of the dependent variable. The key to successfully applying this method is to remember that the output of the equation requires using the mean and standard deviation of the dependent variable (GPA, for this example) to convert the output to its equivalent raw score. The correlation for the raw data shown in Figure 4-1 was computed using SPSS and the output is shown in Tables 4-1 and 4-2, which provides the information needed to apply this method of prediction.

Table 4-1. Descriptive Statistics

	Mean	Std. Deviation	N
GPA	2.142	.8969	12
AdmTest	10.00	4.264	12

Table 4-2. Correlations

		GPA	AdmTest
Pearson Correlation	GPA	1.000	.556
	AdmTest	.556	1.000
Sig. (1-tailed)	GPA		.030
	AdmTest	.030	
N	GPA	12	12
	AdmTest	12	12

To make a prediction using the standardized regression equation, start with the raw score of the variable from which you are predicting and convert this score to a z-score.

$$Z_X = (X - M)/SD = (12 - 10.00)/4.264 = .4690$$

Then, use the standardized regression equation to find the z-score of the variable being predicted.

$$\text{Predicted } Z_Y = (\beta)Z_X$$

Where, β = Pearson correlation.

$$Z_Y = (.556)(.4690) = .2608$$

Convert Z_y to a raw score, if desired, using this equation.

$$Y = (SD_Y)(Z_Y) + M_Y = (.8969)(.2608) + 2.142 = 2.3759,$$ which is within rounding error of the previous results.

Note that assuming a correlation of zero between X and Y would mean that any value of X would result in a predicted z-score of zero for Y, which is equal to the mean of Y. Thus, when the correlation is zero, the predicted value for the dependent variable is always a z-score of zero which equals the mean. The same result would be obtained using the raw score regression equation.

Regression to the Mean

The standardized regression equation illustrates the important concept of **regression to the mean**. Regression to (or toward) the mean is an inevitable statistical phenomenon that occurs because correlations are never perfect. As you can see from the standardized regression equation, the predicted value always moves toward the mean if the correlation is less than 1.00. In fact, the correlation of a measure with *itself* is not even perfect. Such correlations (called reliability coefficients) generally range from .70 to about .95. Regression toward the mean needs to be accounted for in two key situations.

The first is in constructing a **confidence interval** around a test score. The confidence interval is part of a distribution that would result if a test were administered many times to the same person. This application of confidence intervals is used to communicate that a test score (such as the score on an IQ test) represents a range of scores within which future administrations of the test are likely to fall. This prevents confusion for tests that are administered several times to the same person. The confidence interval is the middle 90% or 95% of this distribution. The reliability and the *SD* of the test are used to estimate the characteristics of this hypothetical distribution. For example, consider a child whose IQ score is 130, which is two standard deviations above the mean. IQ scores are very reliable but not perfectly. Thus, the center of the confidence interval is adjusted to account for regression toward the mean because the reliability of the test will be less than perfect. Practically, this means that the center of the confidence interval is regressed toward the mean using the reliability coefficient to predict the child's true score (Nunnally, 1967). For example, assume the reliability of this test is .94, typical for IQ tests. Using the reliability coefficient to predict the child's IQ upon being retested would result in a score of 128.2. In other words, if the same child were tested a second time, their score would be expected to regress toward the mean in proportion to the reliability coefficient of .94. This predicted score would become the center of the confidence interval. The way to find the limits of the confidence interval is to use the **standard error of measurement**. The standard error of measurement is the name for the standard deviation of test scores that would be expected if a test were administered an infinite number of times to the same individual. It represents the variability expected to surround an individual test score. Using the SD of the test and its reliability coefficient, the standard error of measurement can be computed. In this hypothetical case it is equal to 3.67, so the 90% confidence interval would be $128.2 \pm (1.64)(3.67) = 128.2 \pm 6.02$. There is a 90% chance that the child's true score would be between and 122.2 and 134.2. Because regression toward the mean is greatest for very high or very low scores, it can be important when educational placement decisions are made. This topic and the details of computation are covered more thoroughly in tests and measurements courses.

This concept is like the confidence interval for a correlation coefficient which was discussed in Chapter 3. In both cases, the confidence interval communicates the variability associated with a score, in one case a correlation coefficient based upon a sample of many individuals versus the confidence interval around a single person's score. Both applications of confidence intervals focus on the variability associated with data, whether coming from a single person or a large sample.

A second situation where regression to the mean is important is in experimental design. Imagine that a researcher is studying the efficacy of a treatment for depression. If the researcher selects a group of severely depressed people for the study, regression to the mean becomes an important issue, because depression scores, on average, will regress toward the mean when the depressed people are tested a second time. No depression test is perfectly reliable, so the regression toward the mean is an inevitable statistical fact. To provide a fair test of the efficacy of the treatment program, an untreated control group of equally severely depressed individuals is needed. The untreated control group will also regress toward the mean, so proof of the effectiveness of the program is obtained when the treatment group shows more improvement than the control group.

Review Questions for Chapter 4

1. Look at Figure 4-1. If a person has a score of 6 on the Admission Test, what is their predicted GPA?
2. Now use the raw score regression equation to predict GPA from a raw score of 13 on the Admission Test.
3. Use the standardized regression equation to predict GPA from an Admission Test score of 9.
4. If the correlation between X and Y is 0.00, what will be the result of using any value of X to predict Y?
5. What is regression to the mean?

1. $\hat{Y} = 1.65$

2. $.117(13) + .972 = 2.493$

3. $.117(9) + .972 = 2.025$

4. Y will be 0

5. inevitable statistical phenomenon

Answers to Chapter 4 Review Questions

1. about 1.65

2. First, use the raw score regression equation: GPA = .117 (AdminTest) + .972

   Then substitute the value of 13 for AdminTest.

   This results in GPA = .117 (13) + .972 = 2.493

   The predicted value for GPA is 2.493

3. The prediction begins with by converting the raw score of 9 for the Admission Test to a z-score

   $Z_X = (X - M)/SD = (9 - 10.00)/4.264 = -.2345$

   Use the standardized regression equation to find the predicted z-score for GPA
   Predicted $Z_Y = (\beta)Z_X$

   Where, β = Pearson correlation.

   $Z_Y = (.556) (-.2345) = -.1304$

   Convert Z_y to a raw score, if desired, using this equation.

   $Y = (SD_Y) (Z_Y) + M_Y = (.8969) (-.1304) + 2.142 = 2.025$, which is very close to the value that could be read from Figure 4-1.

4. The mean of Y. Use the standardized regression equation (Predicted $Z_Y = (\beta)Z_X$. With a value of zero for beta (β), any value of X will result in a predicted z-score of zero for Y. This is the mean of Y.

5. The predicted value for any situation will move toward the mean because correlations are not perfect.

Chapter 5: Important Concepts for Statistical Thinking

This chapter reviews key terms and concepts that contribute to understanding the logic of statistical inference and how to choose the appropriate statistical test for common research scenarios.

Population versus Sample

The process of inferential statistics involves making inferences from samples to populations. The sample is the group of observations that the research has. The population is the larger group from which the sample comes and to which the results from the sample are expected to apply. When a statistically significant result is obtained, this is evidence that the result applies to a larger population.

Statistical tests are based on distributions with known properties, like a normal curve, which makes it possible to determine the probability of the values on that distribution (e.g., t-distribution, F-distribution, etc.). For the inferences made from these statistics to be accurate, assumptions need to be made about the distribution of scores in the *population*. This is where the term parametric statistics comes from. It means that assumptions are made about the population distribution of the variables.

Assumptions apply to the populations, not the samples. For example, imagine a researcher is doing an independent groups t-test. One of the assumptions is that the population variances for the two groups are homogeneous. To calculate the t-test, variances from each sample are combined to obtain the best estimate of the characteristics of the distribution of differences between means, the comparison distribution for an independent groups t-test. Because two sample variances are combined, the variances of the *samples* are not expected to be exactly the same. There will typically be a difference that would naturally result from taking independent samples from a population. It is an inferential statistics question as to whether it is reasonable to assume that the two sample variances came from the same population. Levene's test for homogeneity of variances, which is part of the SPSS output for the independent groups t-test, is one way to answer this question. If the results of Levene's test are statistically significant, the variances are assumed to have come from different populations, violating the assumption. When testing the assumptions of a parametric test, a statistically significant result is bad news because it indicates the assumption has been violated.

A population is the entire group of scores or people to which a researcher intends that the results will apply. This is critical knowledge, especially when the research describes a psychological or medical treatment. On the other hand, the exact population to which the results might apply can be ambiguous and intensely debated. One reason is that many studies involve convenience samples such as students from introductory psychology classes who participate in research as part of a course requirement or the people who responded to an online survey. Note that ethical standards require availability of an alternate means of meeting the course requirement, and the right of any participant to refuse to participate in any research or withdraw from the research at any time, cannot be compromised by any research protocol. Assuming a study draws its participants from introductory psychology classes, what population is represented by such a sample?

This question is complex because the answer depends upon so many variables. Where is the institution located? Is it public or private? Is it small or large? What ethnic groups are represented? What is the typical age of the participants? What admission criteria does the institution use? Does the institution have a liberal arts focus? Are students recruited regionally or nationally? Are international students represented? Once these questions and more are answered, the researcher can create a reasonable, though never complete, profile of the population from which the subjects are presumed to have come. Because there are so many possible variations in the profile of the population, it is challenging to precisely specify the population for any given study. This is one reason that successful **replication** of research findings can be difficult; a subtle difference between populations, which is not yet understood to be important, could alter research outcomes. When results do not replicate (i.e., produce the same results when they are repeated), heated discussions can occur among the researchers as they try to interpret the pattern of findings. When researchers discuss the weaknesses of their studies, an issue that frequently arises is the representativeness of the sample, and replication of the study in other populations is a common suggestion for future research. In sum, for most research studies, precisely defining the population is a challenging task.

There are situations where the population can be specified with good precision. Students attending a single school, college, or university; members of a specific organization; psychology majors at one institution; or prospective graduate students who take a particular admission test are examples of such groups. Because there is a complete list of people who are members of these populations, it is possible to obtain good samples that represent these populations very well.

To summarize, a population is the larger group of individuals to which research findings are expected to apply. A sample is a subset of the population; the sample is the group of individuals who participate in a study. Research is performed on a sample and the results are expected to apply to the population represented by the sample. The term **inferential statistics** is used to describe the fact that samples of populations are used to make inferences about the population from which the sample was derived.

Random Sample
If a population can be specified with good precision, a sample can be obtained that represents the population extremely well. One way to do this is by taking a **random sample**. A random sample begins with a list of the entire population, and then the sample is drawn from the population in a way the gives each member of the population an equal chance to be selected. This is an ideal method of obtaining a sample and guarantees that the sample accurately represents the target population. Realistically, random sampling is rarely accomplished. One problem is that some randomly selected subjects will refuse to participate which is their legal and ethical right. It is also extremely difficult to obtain a list of an entire population from which one can select. Instead, researchers try to obtain a **representative sample** using other methods. The main method is to ensure that important groups are represented in proportion to their presence in the population, often using the US census as the basic guide. This is a topic that will be thoroughly covered in most research methods courses, but no matter how deeply one goes into the topic of obtaining samples from populations, to a large extent, researchers use convenience samples of individuals who are available to study. These convenience samples can vary widely in the diversity of participants. Some samples have a narrow range of diversity whereas other samples include individuals from a variety of cultures, income levels, and family backgrounds. The greater the diversity of participants in the sample, the broader the population represented.

One key to understanding inferential statistics is to comprehend that the group one studies is a sample of a broader population to which the results are expected to apply. In order for results to apply to a diverse population, the sample must include a diverse group of individuals that reflects the diversity of the population. However, a sample represents some population, even if it is not well-specified. It is this larger group of participants who were not included in the study to which the results are expected to apply. The statistical outcomes provide the evidence of whether a sample result can be expected to apply in a larger population.

Measured versus Manipulated Variables
This concept is strongly related to **independent** and **dependent** variables, which are defined below. A **manipulated** variable is controlled by the researcher, and, thus, has a causal relationship with the dependent variable (if the study is successful). If the subjects are **randomly assigned** to groups, the variable is clearly manipulated. Random assignment means that each person in the study has an equal chance or probability of being assigned to a group or condition. This is an essential concept in research. If a researcher has been able to manipulate a variable through random assignment, it will be mentioned several times in the article. Although random *assignment* and random *selection* are similar sounding terms, they are very different. Random selection is an ideal way of obtaining subjects that is rarely accomplished in practice. Random assignment is done after subjects are recruited to participate in a study. It is a way of assigning subjects to groups or conditions that assures equality of the groups before the study begins. It is an essential element of true experiments in which a variable is manipulated. There are a few other ways to manipulate a variable, discussed in advanced courses. The dependent variable in a true experiment is a measured variable. The most important indicator that a variable is manipulated is random assignment. If random assignment is not present, the variable is measured. For example, gender is a measured variable because there is no way to randomly assign people to be male or female. On the

other hand, there might be ways to manipulate gender. One option is to construct three sets of identical job applications and have a picture of a female with one set of applications, a picture of a male with another set, and a picture of a person with ambiguous gender in a third set. Then, subjects can be asked to evaluate one of the applications. In this case, subjects can be randomly assigned to receive an application with a male or a female or an ambiguous picture attached to it. The type of picture would be a manipulated variable. The ratings of the applications would be a measured (not manipulated) variable. Morling (2018) uses this vocabulary to structure her research methods textbook.

A very important type of measured variable is psychological or medical diagnosis. It is not possible to randomly assign people to have a disorder such as depression, cancer, schizophrenia, MS, OCD, ADD, etc. Thus, the most important variables studied by psychologists and medical researchers are typically measured. On the other hand, it is possible to take a group of people diagnosed with a disorder such as severe anxiety, BPD, or cancer, and randomly assign them to treatment groups to test the efficacy of various treatments. The type of treatment would be a manipulated variable.

Random Assignment
Random assignment means to use a process that guarantees each subject in a study has an equal chance to be assigned to each group. For example, assume that a study has an experimental group and a control group. One way to ensure random assignment is to flip a coin to establish the condition to which each subject will be assigned. Another common method of random assignment is to use a **table of random numbers**. Random assignment can be used only when the researcher has control of the variable so that it can be manipulated. Use of a manipulated variable with random assignment to groups is a necessary condition to make a causal inference or claim that the independent variable causes the dependent variable. Often random assignment is done with a requirement that equal number of subjects be assigned to each experimental group in the study. Ensuring equal numbers of subjects in the groups makes doing and interpreting statistical analyses easier.

Whereas true random *samples* are difficult to obtain for a variety of reasons, assignment of subject to groups must be done randomly whenever possible. It is required that the researcher randomly assign people to different conditions in a true experiment with a manipulated variable. An example is a study in which subjects can receive either an active medication or an identical-looking placebo that does not contain the active medication. Studies like this must use random assignment to ensure that the groups are equal at the beginning of the study. Random assignment means to assign subjects to groups so there is an equal chance of assignment to each group. For example, a coin flip or table of random numbers could be used to decide whether each subject receives the placebo or the active medication. The result is a very strong experimental design that allows one to infer that the independent variable *causes* any differences that are found. When reading published research articles, it is important to assess whether the researcher used random assignment which will always be clearly stated in the methods section and elsewhere in the article.

There is a caveat regarding studies that use random assignment. Although a successful study with random assignment provides strong evidence that a causal relationship exists between the manipulated variable and the measured dependent variable, it would be preferable to see a replication or repeat of the results to strengthen the causal claim. It has proven more difficult than anticipated to replicate studies (e.g., Cumming, 2013; Ioannidis, 2005). Thus, a single study, even if the independent variable was manipulated with random assignment, may not be sufficient evidence to support a causal claim.

Research with Measured Variables
The use of preexisting or measured variables in research is very common because many variables that are interesting to study cannot be manipulated. Gender, diagnosis, personality, intelligence, academic performance, genetics, and reaction time, are a few examples of variables that can be measured but not manipulated. Measured variables can be used to place subjects into groups or as independent variables in correlation or multiple regression studies. Correlations or group differences found with measured variables do not provide direct evidence of a causal relationship. Instead, they indicate an association between or among the measured variables has been identified. Associations are sometimes the only evidence that can be gathered for variables that are important to study such as diseases or genetic conditions. Thus, researchers need to be aware that causal claims can be made when from evidence based upon associations. Multiple regression is a statistical technique that allows a researcher to control or eliminate confounding variables to

strengthen a causal claim. Furthermore, a multitude of findings supporting a causal claim can arise from studies that use measured variables. Thus, the study of variables that can be measured but not manipulated can make a strong contribution to the scientific literature.

Summary

To summarize, random sampling is a method of obtaining subjects for a study. If a list of population members can be obtained, random sampling or selection ensures that the population is represented well and that results of the study can be expected to apply to the entire population. Unfortunately, random selection is difficult to do because complete lists of populations are difficult to find, and potential participants have the legal and ethical right to refuse to participate if they are selected.

Random assignment is a method of assigning participants to groups after the sample has been obtained. Each participant has an equal chance of being assigned to a group. It is an essential procedure in true experiments. Random assignment assures that the groups in an experiment are equal before the procedure is conducted. Then, the obtained differences can be attributed to the manipulated variable. If the author of a study claims to have done an experiment and makes a causal claim, random assignment must be used to place subjects into groups. When random assignment is used, the researcher has a manipulated variable and can make a causal claim that the independent variable causes changes in the dependent variable. However, it is important to replicate the study to strengthen the causal claim. When a measured variable is used to divide participants into groups, the result is a weaker design that establishes an association between the variables but does not establish causation. Much more evidence would be required to support a causal claim.

Independent and Dependent Variables

The terms **independent variable** and **dependent variable** are thoroughly studied in research methods and advanced statistics courses. These terms are also extremely useful descriptive terms that assist in identifying the correct statistical procedure. Thus, the terms are covered in *QRST* but not in the same detail as will occur in more advanced courses.

The *APA Dictionary of Psychology* (American Psychological Association, 2007) defines an independent variable as "the variable in an experiment that is specifically manipulated or is observed to occur before the occurrence of the dependent, or outcome, variable. Independent variables may or may not be causally related to the dependent variable. In statistical analysis, an independent variable is likely to be referred to as a predictor variable" (p. 475). A dependent variable is defined as "the 'outcome' variable that is observed to occur or change after the occurrence or variation of the independent variable. Dependent variables may or may not be related causally to the independent variable" (p. 269).

It is easy to identify the independent variable in a true experiment. The independent variable is the variable that has been manipulated by the researcher. For example, in an experiment in which the effect of a placebo versus active medication upon reaction time is studied, the independent variable is clearly "medication vs. placebo" and the dependent variable is reaction time. In any test of differences, the variable used to place subjects into groups is considered an independent variable and it does not matter whether the variable is manipulated by the researcher (i.e., has random assignment) or is measured. Thus, "active medication versus placebo" and gender are both considered independent variables because they result in different groups of subjects.

A grey area is correlation. It is often not clear what variable(s) should be labeled independent and dependent in a bivariate correlational study because neither variable is manipulated. For example, in a study correlating GPA and IQ, it is not clear what causes what. Does IQ cause GPA or does the learning associated with GPA influence IQ? On the other hand, in a study correlating "study hours" and college GPA, it is likely that the researcher would label study hours the independent variable and college GPA the dependent variable because studying is most likely to cause GPA. However, the opposite is a possibility. Perhaps grades are a reward for studying and the true direction of causality is that GPA causes study hours. In sum, labeling the dependent variable and independent variable in a bivariate correlation study is done logically, but there is always a risk that the labeling is incorrect because neither variable is manipulated.

Fortunately, in *multiple* regression, convention takes over, and the labels are clear. Multiple regression involves having more than one variable simultaneously predicting one other variable. In this case, the predictor variables are labeled independent variables, and the variable being predicted is the dependent variable.

It is essential to understand these labels as you progress through courses beyond introductory statistics. They are indispensable in the vocabulary of research and data analysis.

Replication

Replication means to repeat a study or do it again. It has proven difficult to replicate results of many published studies (Ioannidis, 2005; Open Science Collaboration, 2015). For example, an attempt to replicate 97 psychological studies found that only 35 of the studies were successfully replicated (Open Science Collaboration, 2015). Studies that fail to replicate present a profound challenge to the process of statistical analysis. If results do not replicate, what is the purpose of using statistical analysis? The main purpose of statistical analysis is to seek evidence that the results of a sample apply to the larger population. If the information gained from a study is not repeatable, the treatments that the studies support, and our understanding of human behavior are perhaps based upon false information. In my opinion, the situation is not as dire as some writers would have us believe. However, replication may be one of the most neglected sources of supporting evidence for causal claims and developing our understanding of human behavior. Consequently, researchers need to understand the conditions that increase the likelihood of a failure to be able to replicate a study. This issue will be covered frequently throughout the remainder of *QRST*.

To assess your understanding of the concepts in this chapter, a practice exercise is below. Answers are provided on the page following the exercise.

Review of Measured, Manipulated, Independent, and Dependent Variables

For each of the scenarios listed below, identify the independent (IV) and dependent variables (DV) and whether each variable is manipulated or measured. Note: it is challenging to write such scenarios because this vocabulary is so central to the ways research is discussed. It is difficult to write about research without using these terms.

1.   A researcher randomly assigns participants to receive an anxiety medication or placebo and then tests their reaction time in a driving simulator.
a.   What is the independent variable? Is it measured or manipulated (circle one)?

b.   What is the dependent variable? Is it measured or manipulated (circle one)?

2.   A survey researcher is interested in male-female differences in college GPA.
a.   What is the independent variable? Is it measured or manipulated (circle one)?

b.   What is the dependent variable? Is it measured or manipulated (circle one)?

3.   A researcher is interested in the correlation between College GPA and scores on a test measuring attitudes and behavior associated with lifelong learning. The scale is called the Lifelong Learning Scale (LLS).
a.   What is the independent variable? Is it measured or manipulated (circle one)?

b.   What is the dependent variable? Is it measured or manipulated (circle one)?

4.   A researcher is interested in what variables are associated with healthy relationships. She asks a group of 300 women to complete four scales: a Relationship Health Scale, an Empathy scale, a scale of Assertiveness, and a scale of Communication Skills. She then performs a multiple regression using scores on the Empathy, Assertiveness, and Communication scales to predict Relationship Health.
a.   What is/are the independent variable(s)? Is it (they) measured or manipulated (circle one)?

b.   What is the dependent variable? Is it measured or manipulated (circle one)?

5.   A researcher recruits 60 individuals with high blood pressure and then randomly assigns them to three treatment groups which each last six weeks: Mindfulness training, Muscle relaxation training, and a waitlist control group. The blood pressure of all participants is assessed at the beginning of the study and once again six weeks later and the difference scores (Post – pre) are analyzed. Identify the variables in this study and classify each as either measured or manipulated and independent or independent.
a.   Variable 1: Name: _____; Measured vs manipulated (circle one). Independent vs dependent (circle one).
b.   Variable 2: Name: _____; Measured vs manipulated (circle one). Independent vs dependent (circle one).

6.   A researcher is interested in the relationship between height and peer status. She obtains access to a sample of 100 second grade boys and girls and assesses their height, classifying them as short vs. average vs. tall, and their score on a measure of peer popularity developed especially for this study. Identify the variables in this study and classify each as either measure or manipulated and independent or independent.
a.   Variable 1: Name: _____; Measured vs manipulated (circle one). Independent vs dependent (circle one).

b.   Variable 2: Name: _____; Measured vs manipulated (circle one). Independent vs dependent (circle one).
c.   Variable 3: Name: _____; Measured vs manipulated (circle one). Independent vs dependent (circle one).

7.   Twenty students are randomly assigned to a group that receives instruction and practice in computing the *SD*, or a group that receives instruction, but no practice. A test of knowledge of computing the *SD* is administered two weeks later. Identify the variables in this study and classify each as either measured or manipulated and independent or independent.
a.   Variable 1: Name: _____; Measured vs manipulated (circle one). Independent vs dependent (circle one).
b.   Variable 2: Name: _____; Measured vs manipulated (circle one). Independent vs dependent (circle one).

8.   A researcher wants to answer the question of whether height is related to level of sports participation. She surveys a large number of student athletes and identifies three categories of athletes: varsity athletes, intramural athletes, and nonathletes. She also divides the sample by gender. The she measures the height of each individual in the study. Identify the variables in this study and classify each as either measure or manipulated and independent or dependent.
a.   Variable 1: Name: _____; Measured vs manipulated (circle one). Independent vs dependent (circle one).
b.   Variable 2: Name: _____; Measured vs manipulated (circle one). Independent vs dependent (circle one).
c.   Variable 3: Name: _____; Measured vs manipulated (circle one). Independent vs dependent (circle one).

9.   What is the meaning of replication? Why is replication an important component of research?

See the following page for answers to the exercise.

Answers to Chapter 5 Review

1. Independent variable : Medication vs. placebo; manipulated; dependent variable: Reaction time, measured
2. Independent variable: Gender, measured; dependent variable: College GPA, measured
3. Independent variable: Score on lifelong learning test or College GPA; dependent variable: College GPA or Score on lifelong learning test; both variables are measured
4. Independent variable: Empathy, Assertiveness, Communication scores; all measured; dependent variable: Relationship Health, measured
5. Variable 1: Blood pressure difference, measured DV; Variable 2: Type of Training, manipulated independent variable
6. Variable 1: Gender, measured, independent variable; Variable 2: Height, measured, independent variable, Variable 3: Peer Status, measured dependent variable
7. Variable 1: Practice vs. No practice, manipulated, independent variable; Variable 2: Knowledge of *SD*, measured, dependent variable
8. Variable 1: Gender, measured, independent variable; Variable 2: Sports type, measured, independent; Variable 3: Height, measured dependent variable
9. Replication means to do a research study a second time. Studies should be replicated because it strengthens the argument in favor of the treatments that the studies support and our understanding of human behavior. We shouldn't be basing treatments and our understanding of human behavior upon false information.

Chapter 6: Logic of Null Hypothesis Significance Testing (NHST)

One of the most important topics in introductory statistics is the logic of statistical inference. The theoretical literature often uses the term Null Hypothesis Significance Testing and the abbreviation NHST, to describe this logic, so *QRST* will follow that tradition. The logic of statistical inference is complex and filled with argument and controversy and there have been calls to abandon NHST altogether. However, NHST continues to survive and students are expected to know the core logic. Perhaps its survival is related to its pragmatic usefulness and the lack of viable substitutes. If you desire to look more deeply into the logic and controversy surrounding NHST, Howell (2010), Krueger (2001), Nickerson (2000), and Wilkinson et al. (1999) provide good starting points. Two alternatives or supplements to NHST that have received attention are **confidence intervals** and **Bayes Theorem**. However, each alternative has its own weaknesses and neither has fully replaced NHST.

The Core Logic of NHST

One of the learning aids I have developed for my own introductory statistics classes, which uses the textbook by Aron, Coups, and Aron (2011), is a very brief outline of the core logic of null hypothesis significance testing. I had this outline made into a rubber stamp. I stamp the logic into students' notebooks and I use it to evaluate short essays written to demonstrate understanding of the logic. I encourage students to memorize this outline and use it to guide their writing.

> **NHST Logic**
> **Restate as RH, NH re Pops**
> **Assume NH is correct**
> **Low prob of NH, reject NH**
> **Reject NH > support for RH**
> **Power; ES; Type I, II errors**

Below is an expanded version of the same outline.

> **NHST Logic**
> **Restate the problem as a research hypothesis and null hypothesis regarding the populations.**
> **Assume the null hypothesis is correct.**
> **If there is a low probability of the null hypothesis being correct, the null hypothesis is rejected.**
> **Rejection of the null hypothesis implies support for the research hypothesis.**
> **Discuss other concepts such as statistical power, effect size, and Type I and Type II errors.**

Students who are in courses for which they are expected to know and explain the logic of NHST may find it helpful to memorize one of the above outlines. The following sections explain the logic in more detail.

Restate the Problem as a Research Hypothesis, and Null Hypothesis Regarding the Populations

This aspect of NHST is only discussed in introductory statistics classes and almost never in research articles; it is an implied component of the process. The basic process of inferential statistics uses sample data to make inferences about a larger population. Thus, the formal logic of the process is to frame the problem in terms of populations. Imagine that a study evaluates the effect of a new psychological treatment for anxiety. In a simple experiment, this would result in two populations. One population is people who might receive the treatment, and the other is people like those in the control group who do not receive the treatment. By conducting the study, the researcher is seeking evidence that the "treatment" had a positive effect on the sample and that the results obtained for the sample can be expected to generalize to the population of individuals who may receive the treatment in the future.

After the populations have been defined, the next step is to make up null and research hypotheses about them. The null hypothesis assumes a zero or null effect in the research study. If the study is looking at differences, the null hypothesis would be that the populations are the same (i.e., have the same mean). The research hypothesis is the opposite and typically states that the populations are different, which implies a two-tailed test. A one-tailed test would specify a direction for the difference. However, one-tailed tests are so rarely allowed in published research that they are ignored in *QRST*. If the research involves a correlation coefficient, the two populations are people for whom the variables are not related and people like those in the study. The null hypothesis is that the populations are the same which means there is no relationship between the variables.

Assume the Null Hypothesis is Correct

This is another component of NHST that is implied but never discussed in research articles. Assuming the null hypothesis is correct means that the research is conducted under the assumption that there is no difference or effect in the study. This is the *opposite* of what the researcher really believes, and there have been reams written about the use of this logic in NHST. One advantage of assuming the null to be correct is that it allows researchers to work with distributions with known characteristics. Since characteristics of the distribution are known, the probability of obtaining a particular sample can be found. The comparison distribution can be a normal distribution, *t*-distribution, *F*-distribution, chi square, or other distribution.

If there is a Low Probability of Obtaining the Research Results by Chance, the Null Hypothesis is rejected

Finally, we come to the public part of the NHST process. It is forbidden to mention the null hypothesis in a research article, but probabilities are scattered everywhere in the results section. For each result, the researcher reports the probability of obtaining that result through chance or random variation, assuming the null hypothesis is true. When there is a low probability of obtaining the sample value, the null hypothesis is rejected.

The comparison distribution is used to determine the probability. If the probability is less than alpha, which is almost always set at .05, the null hypothesis is rejected. The language used in the typical research article is to describe the result as either "statistically significant" when the null hypothesis was rejected, or "not significant" or "not statistically significant" or "NS" when the null hypothesis was not rejected.

If a large number of statistical tests are presented in a table, there are several ways to indicate which results are statistically significant (i.e., the null hypothesis was rejected). One method is to show the exact probability of obtaining the sample result for each test. Then the reader needs to examine each result and determine which ones are greater than or less than .05. For example, if it says "$p = .001$," this is clearly less than .05, so the result *is* statistically significant. Another option is to report either $p > .05$ (the probability is greater than .05, therefore not statistically significant), or $p < .05$ (the probability is less than .05, therefore it *is* statistically significant). Often, the probability is replaced with *NS* when the result is not statistically significant. Another common method of indicating statistical significance is to place asterisks next to the result to indicate the probability with a key at the bottom of the table. Results without an asterisk are not statistically significant.

In sum, the probability of obtaining the sample result through chance or random variation, assuming the null hypothesis is correct, is used to judge whether the null hypothesis is rejected. The focus of research articles is on presenting the probability without any attention to the context of NHST logic. It is assumed that the reader has thorough knowledge of NHST, so journal space is not used to review this. However, it is critical to remember the meaning of the probabilities presented throughout an empirical article. They show the probability that the results were due to chance or random variation assuming the null hypothesis is correct. When the probability is low (less than .05) the null hypothesis is rejected, and the results support the researcher's hypothesis.

Rejection of the Null Hypothesis implies support for the Research Hypothesis

This is the last step in NHST logic. If the null hypothesis is rejected, the researcher now has evidence that the original hypothesis that inspired the research has been supported. Although this is very good news, most researchers focus on the probabilities provided by the statistical output; they don't think or write about the null hypothesis and how it is related to their research hypothesis. At this point NHST logic has come to a full circle. It begins with a research idea that is translated into a research and null hypothesis about the populations. Then the null hypothesis is assumed to be correct. If the probability of the null hypothesis being correct is low enough (< .05), the null hypothesis is rejected, and the research hypothesis is supported.

Almost inevitably, there is a difference between sample means or a non-zero correlation. The statistical question is whether the difference is large enough to infer that the difference exists in the entire population. The process of inferential statistics makes inferences about populations. When we declare a result statistically significant, we are claiming that the result is valid for the entire population represented by the sample. In other words, the treatment not only worked for the sample, but it also will work in the future when other members of the population are either created by giving them the treatment or sampled from a preexisting population. Statistical significance does not mean that the magnitude of the difference or relationship is nontrivial or meaningful. In fact, with a large enough sample size, almost any difference, no matter how small or trivial, may be statistically significant. This is one of the major criticisms of NHST. This criticism can be effectively addressed by looking at the effect size and power of the study.

The null hypothesis is not discussed in articles reporting original research results. Instead, results are described as statistically significant (NH was rejected) or not statistically significant (NH was not rejected). However, null hypothesis significance testing is the underlying logic. When a result is statistically significant, the null hypothesis was rejected because the probability of getting that result by chance or through random variation was so small that it makes the null hypothesis (of no difference) untenable. In sum, when the probability of obtaining the given result by chance or through random variation is low (almost always less than .05), the null hypothesis is rejected, and the research hypothesis is supported.

A key concept is the word *supported,* which is a very deliberate word choice. The research hypothesis is "supported," not proven, because the entire logic of NHST is based upon probability. Consequently, there is no certainty. The concepts of Type I and Type II errors, described in subsequent sections, elaborate on the nature of the uncertainty.

The term *research hypothesis* appears frequently in scientific writing, but the context is typically the introduction or discussion sections of the article, not the results section. Many research journals require that the writer present a series of hypotheses about the expected outcome of their research. These hypotheses are presented in the paper's introduction. These same hypotheses are then reviewed in the discussion section, which comes after the results section. Although this use of the term research hypothesis has links to NHST logic, the discussion takes place outside this context.

Type I Errors

There are two kinds of statistical errors, brilliantly named Type I and Type II errors. It is the possibility of these errors that makes the outcomes of a scientific experiment tentative and the reason that we state the research hypothesis was "supported." A **Type I error** means that the null hypothesis has been rejected when the populations really don't differ. This could be described as a **false positive**. Even if the populations are identical, there is a chance of rejecting the null, which is equal to alpha (usually .05), because five percent of the scores in the comparison distribution will fall beyond the cutoff points. If the sample comes from these areas, the null will be rejected even if the populations do not differ at all. The only way to make a Type I error less likely is to use a lower alpha level such as .01 or .001. This strategy is not used very often because the result is an increase in the probability of making a Type II error. Instead, we depend upon later attempts to repeat or replicate results to separate true differences from Type I errors. In sum, a Type I error is when the NH was rejected when it should not have been rejected. The chances of a Type I error are equal to alpha or 5% *assuming the NH is correct*. However, if the NH is not true, which is the case when the experimental evidence leads to its rejection, the probability that the results represent a Type I error can be much lower than the set alpha level (Nickerson, 2000). As experimental evidence in favor of a theory accumulates, attributing the results to a Type I error is less arguable. Type I errors can be difficult to identify because they require replication of the original study and, at the same time, successful replication makes a Type I error less likely.

Thus, the process of NHST guarantees that 5% of initial findings will be false and fail to replicate in future studies. This means that a potential failure to be replicated is built in to any initial research finding. Later, it will be shown how the concepts of statistical power and effect size can help us predict when replication is likely to be problematic.

Type II Errors

Type II errors occur when the null hypothesis is not rejected when it should be rejected because the populations actually differ. This could be described as a **false negative**. The main reason Type II errors occur is because the study was lacking in statistical power (see the next section). The main method of increasing statistical power is to have more subjects in the study. Type II errors may be more important than Type I errors because a Type II error could result in an important potential finding (such as an effective cure or treatment for a disease) being ignored. There are numerous ways to decrease the chances of a Type II error, but the most important one is to *get more subjects*. Effect size (ES) provides a way of estimating whether the effort of obtaining more subjects would be useful. If the effect size is small or very small, it may not be worth the effort of obtaining enough subjects to increase statistical power to an adequate level. By looking at previous studies, it is possible to estimate the effect size likely to be obtained in a new research study. Alternately, the study could be designed around the assumption that a certain effect size (e.g., small, medium, or large) is desirable to detect. This information can be used for estimating the number of subjects needed in the new study. Many textbooks such as Aron, Coups, and Aron (2011) provide tables answering this question. Alternately, searching the Internet for "sample size calculator" will lead to several online programs for estimating the number of subjects needed to reach 80% power.

Statistical Power

Statistical power is the *probability* of *not* making a Type II error. The opposite of statistical power is beta (β), which is the probability that a Type II error will be made. A Type II error results when the populations are different, and the study did not produce a statistically significant result because the sample mean did not differ enough from the control group to cause the null hypothesis to be rejected. Statistical power is the probability of *not* having a Type II error ($1 - \beta$). Cohen (1992) argues that studies should be designed to have power of .80 or 80 percent. This means that 80% of the experimental group lies beyond the cutoff. With 80% power, there is an 80% chance of drawing a sample from the experimental population that lies beyond the cutoff, so the null hypothesis is rejected. Even with 80% power, there is still a 20% chance of drawing a sample that does not lie beyond the cutoff, so the null hypothesis is not rejected. That is why we say *the results are inconclusive* when the null is not rejected. A Type II error or false negative may have occurred. The main method of increasing power is to increase the number of participants (i.e., get more subjects). Another important variable in determining statistical power is the effect size, discussed in the section that follows.

Figures 6-1 and 6-2 illustrate the concept of statistical power. Each figure shows a hypothetical study involving a control and an experimental condition. The goal of the study is to show that a new treatment will cause happiness scores to be higher. The distribution on the left is the control or no-treatment condition and the one on the right is the experimental condition. Imagine that the distribution on the left represent scores on a happiness scale for a representative sample of the U.S. population. To the extent that the hypothetical therapeutic treatment works, scores on the happiness scale will be higher. If the mean of Happiness scores for the treatment group falls in either the lower 2.5% (bad news) or upper 2.5% (good news; the treatment worked) of the control population, the null hypothesis would be rejected, providing support for the research hypothesis if it was in the upper 2.5%. Note, that 2.5% + 2.5% = 5.0% or .05. Both ends of the distribution are included because a two-tailed test is the norm for research. A statistically significant difference in the opposite direction expected by the researchers suggests a thorough review and revision of the theory used to develop the treatment is needed.

Figure 6-1 illustrates statistical power when the sample mean falls just beyond the cutoff point for the upper 2.5% of the distribution, which would be a statistically significant result. The two distributions shown in the figure represent the population distributions for a generic experiment consisting of an experimental and a control group with a relatively small sample size. In this situation, statistical power is about 50% because half of the distribution for the experimental group is located beyond the cutoff and half is located on the other side of the cutoff. Consequently, an attempt to replicate the experiment under the same circumstances would have about a 50% chance of statistical success because there is about a 50% chance of drawing a second sample from the population that falls beyond the cutoff point. This point is incredibly consequential in the context of replicating the study in the future. If the study was repeated under the same conditions, that is, nothing was done to improve statistical power, the probability of failure is about 50%. At least some of the difficulty in replicating studies comes from this situation, contributing to the "replication crisis."

Figure 6-1. When the cutoff for statistical significance and the mean of the experimental group are close to each other, power is approximately 50%. That is, there is about a 50/50 chance of drawing a sample from the experimental group that falls beyond the cutoff, because about half of the experimental group is beyond the cutoff.

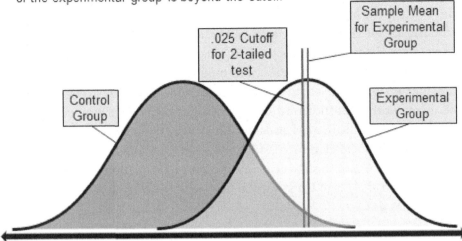

Figure 6-2 illustrates what happens when the sample size has been increased. This causes the distributions' variability to decrease, creating less overlap. In this case, most of the experimental population is beyond the cutoff so that almost any sample from this population would be beyond the cutoff. Although there are other methods for increasing statistical power, by far the most common and probably the easiest is to increase the sample size.

Figure 6-2. When statistical power is increased with a larger sample size, the variation of each group decreases so there is less overlap of the two distributions. With less overlap, almost all of the experimental group is located beyond the cutoff for statistical significance and power is close to 100%. That is, almost any sample from the experimental population will fall beyond the cutoff.

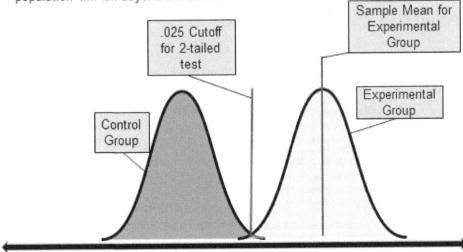

An examination of Figures 6-1 and 6-2 can be used to illustrate important principles of both confidence intervals and replication. Interestingly, the distribution used to illustrate statistical power has the same mean and standard deviation as the distribution from which confidence intervals for the mean are derived. In other words, a confidence interval for the sample mean could be derived by indicating the middle 95% of the distribution that illustrates statistical power. Statisticians who pay attention to effect size and power are aware of the variability inherent in the results for the sample and of the danger of over-interpreting the stability of the sample mean. This is particularly important when the sample mean is located close to the .05 (two-tailed) cutoff. In fact, it applies to any analysis for which the obtained probability is close to the .05 cutoff, such as .049 or .048. In any case where the probability is close to .05 (even if it is slightly above .05), the statistical power is close to .50 or 50%. This means that replication of the study with the same sample size has approximately a 50% chance of failure because half of the distribution for the sample mean is located below the cutoff, where the NH fails to be rejected. The attempt to replicate 97 psychological studies by the Open Science Collaboration (2015) found that "reproducibility success was correlated with indicators of the strength of initial evidence, such as lower original P values and larger effect sizes" (p. aac4716-6), which are both associated with more statistical power. If a researcher has an initial finding for which the p-value is close to .05 (i.e., .04), there is about a 50% chance that an attempt to reproduce the findings will fail unless the researcher increases the power of the study by increasing the number of subjects. This increases the statistical power and makes the confidence interval narrower or more precise. However, when the p-value is close to .05, there is also a possibility that the result is a Type I error (a false positive), and that increasing statistical power will not lead to successful replication of the original result. On the other hand, if the situation is like that shown in Figure 6-2, with statistical power close to 1.0 or 100%, the odds of successful replication are much higher. In fact, a detailed analysis of the statistical power could reveal that the study could be successfully replicated with a smaller sample size.

Effect Size

Effect size is a major factor in statistical power. In tests of differences, effect size is the degree of separation of the populations in standard deviation units. For instance, imagine that the two distributions in Figure 6-1 were pushed further apart. The further the two distributions were from each other, the less overlap, and the greater the effect size. Effect size is computed using the population of individual scores, so it is not influenced by sample size. The bigger the effect size, the more power the study has, because the farther apart the populations are, the less overlap, and the more likely any sample from the treatment population will be beyond the cutoff. A large effect size is good because it means the phenomenon under study is strong and robust. However, small effect sizes can be very important as illustrated by Meyer et al. (2001). The downside is that it can take close to a thousand participants to reach 80% power for studies with small anticipated effect sizes. For some research, this is not practical. Thus, as several writers have argued, many psychological studies may have failed to contribute to general knowledge because they were underpowered. On the other hand, some studies (e.g., large surveys) have so much power, that almost any difference or correlation will be statistically significant. In these cases, it is very helpful to look at the effect size to see how important the result is. Furthermore, the probability of the result (e.g., p = .000) may be very impressive while the effect size is not.

The Effect size (ES) provides critical information for understanding research. ES measures provide information about the strength of a relationship or the magnitude of a difference. When the ES measure provides information about the strength of a relationship, it is reported as a correlation coefficient, squared correlation coefficient, or something similar. Cohen's (as cited in Aron, Coups, & Aron, 2011) effect size conventions for the correlation coefficient (not squared) are .10 for a small effect size, .30 for a medium effect size, and .50 for a large effect size. When the ES measures the strength of a difference, it is reported in standard deviation units relative to the distribution(s) of individual scores. Consequently, it is not affected by the sample size. Cohen's (as cited in Aron, Coups, & Aron, 2011) effect size conventions for mean differences are .2 for a small effect size, .5 for a medium effect size, and .8 for a large effect size.

Effect size measures can be categorized into three groups. Most students learn about the *SD* type of effect size measure first. An *SD* type effect size measure gives the effect size in terms of standard deviation units. That is, the effect size tells how apart the groups are in terms of the standard deviation of the population of individual scores. The second type of effect size measure is the Pearson correlation coefficient which is a measure of effect size. Thus, when reporting correlation coefficients there is no need to report a separate effect size because the correlation coefficient itself is an effect size measure. The third category of effect size measure is variance accounted for or r^2 measures. Recall from Chapter 3 that a squared correlation coefficient provides a measure of variance accounted for or shared variance. This general concept has been used to create several measures of effect size that are particularly useful in analysis of variance and multiple regression. Table 6-1 summarizes common *ES* measures for various statistical procedures.

Table 6-1. Summary of Statistical Procedures and Their Effect Size Measures			
Statistic	**ES Measure**	**Type**	**Small, Medium, Large ES**
Correlation coefficient	R	r	.10, .30, .50
Dependent Means t-test	$M_{diff}/ S_{diff\ scores}$	SD	.20, .50, .80
Independent Means t-test	$(M_1 - M_2)/S_p$, d	SD	.20, .50, .80
Analysis of Variance	S_M/S_{within}	SD	.10, .25, .40
Analysis of Variance	eta-squared (η^2)	r^2	.01, .06, .14
Analysis of Variance	omega-squared (ω^2)	r^2	.01, .06, .14
Chi-square test of indep 2 X 2	phi (Φ) coefficient	r	.10, .30, .50
Chi-square test of indep > 2 X 2	Cramer's phi (Φ) coefficient	r	varies with df for smaller dimension

Knowledge of effect sizes and statistical significance can add greatly to one's ability to interpret and understand a research article. Results showing large effect sizes are generally more meaningful than results with smaller effect sizes. Large effect sizes indicate that the result will be more likely to replicate in future studies and that the result has greater practical importance. A result with a large or very large effect size may be worth a closer look, even if the difference or relationship fails to reach statistical significance. The best way to address this situation would be to obtain more subjects. On the other hand, results with very small effect sizes, obtained in studies with very large sample sizes, may not have much practical importance, may be difficult to replicate, and could mean that the null hypothesis is correct.

Recently, a controversy has emerged regarding the difficulty of replicating (repeating) results of published studies. For example, an attempt to replicate 97 psychological studies found that only 35 of the studies were successfully replicated (Open Science Collaboration, 2015). However, it was also found that "reproducibility success was correlated with indicators of the strength of initial evidence, such as lower original P values and larger effect sizes" (p. aac4716-6). In other words, the stronger the original effect, the more likely it was to be successfully reproduced. Thus, students pursuing their own research projects should keep in mind the value of designing their research with the maximum amount of statistical power that they can afford, while taking additional steps to maximize the effect size. Other things being equal, a researcher would be better off to pursue research projects that show low p values and larger effect sizes. If a researcher is doing a replication plus extension in which the original effect is replicated while other variables are added to the study to look at other questions or interactions, they should carefully examine the original study and conduct a power analysis to estimate as closely as possible the number of subjects needed to have adequate statistical power. If the original study resulted in probabilities close to the .05 cutoff (two-tailed), more subjects than the original study would be prudent.

Effect size is critically important for understanding results and predicting the likelihood of being able to successfully replicate a result in future studies. However, it is challenging, though not impossible, to increase effect size. One way to increase effect size is to increase the intensity of a manipulation. For example, a study of studying techniques could be designed to allow more study time for participants which could increase the effect size and, in turn, statistical power. Increasing the intensity of a manipulation is not always possible or practical. Another technique of increasing effect size is to decrease the variability in the populations. This requires a less diverse more homogeneous sample which may not be compatible with the goals of the research. In sum, there are ways to manipulate effect size, but they can be challenging and impractical. A more practical approach to increasing statistical power is to run any study with the maximum practical sample size.

QRST has provided a basic introduction to a key set of concepts that are important for thinking about statistical results. However, there are too many different tests and too many ways of reporting results to cover everything. Two references that can fill the gaps in your knowledge are Vogt (1999) and Grimm and Yarnold (1995, 2000). For more technical descriptions, see Howell (2010), Tabachnick and Fidell (2013), Grissom and Kim (2012), and Mertler and Vannatta (2013).

You can assess your knowledge of NHST by taking the quiz on the next page. Answers are provided.

Self-Assessment Quiz

1. The hypothesis that there is no difference or no relationship is called _____.
2. The null hypothesis is rejected because _____.
3. Rejection of the null hypothesis implies _____ for the research hypothesis.
4. The probability of a _____ is equal to alpha.
5. A _____ error has occurred when the NH is rejected but the RH is actually false.
6. A _____ error occurs when the researcher fails to reject the NH when the RH is actually true.
7. Generally, researchers should be more concerned about avoiding _____ than _____.
8. When alpha is changed from .05 to .001, the probability of a _____ has been decreased.
9. When alpha is changed from .05 to .001, the probability of a _____ has been increased.
10. When an important empirical study in which you are involved is not "statistically significant," one of the best strategies is to _____.
11. Cohen argues that empirical studies should have statistical power greater than _____.
12. A study with a large effect size and results that are not statistically significant, probably has _____ power.
13. A study with 10,000 participants is likely to have _____ power, but interpretation of the results must be done with caution because statistically significant results that have _____ effect sizes are likely to occur.
14. The two most essential points in the logic of NHST are _____ and _____.
15. A study reporting a statistically significant result with $p = .049$, is likely to have about _____ power. This means that _____.

Answers are on the next page.

Answers:
1. the NH
2. the probability of it being correct is low
3. support
4. Type I error
5. Type I error
6. Type II error
7. Type II errors/Type I errors
8. Type I error
9. Type II error
10. A get more subjects
11. .80 or 80%
12. inadequate or low
13. high/small
14. low probability leads to rejection of the NH/ rejection of the NH provides support for the RH
15. 50% power; there is only a 50-50 chance that the results will be replicated with the same number of subjects.

Chapter 7: Choosing the Correct Test

This chapter covers how to choose the appropriate test given a description of the data to be analyzed or the research design. This prepares you for advanced courses and will enable you to do research projects on your own. Graduate statistics courses are likely to assume that you already have this skill and then build upon it by adding more statistical procedures to those that you already know. Learning to choose the appropriate test also trains you to think critically about interpretation and analysis of research. Deciding which test to use is a complex critical thinking task, because there are so many variables to consider at the same time.

The process of choosing the correct statistical test begins with solid knowledge of statistical tests and recognizing the characteristics of a problem or research situation. One thing I have learned from decades of statistical consulting is that recognizing what statistical test is needed in any situation is critical. If I recognize what the situation calls for, I can look up how to do it. If I don't know the name of the procedure for which the situation calls, I am faced with a more difficult problem. I have summarized the decision process in six steps but there are other ways of approaching this critical thinking task.

1. Read the problem or summarize the research situation carefully. Frequently, a problem needs to be read or reviewed several times to identify the important details. At this step, mastery of vocabulary is important because it provides a way to label key characteristics of a problem or research scenario. These concepts play a key role in the process: dependent variable, independent variable, grouping variable, nominal variable, quantitative variable, and **repeated measure** (see below).

2. Determine the independent (first, causal, or grouping) variable(s) and the dependent (second, measured) variable. See Chapter 5 for a review of this vocabulary, which is essential for discussing data analysis and research design. The absence of a grouping variable is important information and indicates that the problem is likely to involve a test of relationships such as correlation or multiple regression.

3. Determine the level of measurement for each variable in the design. It is also useful to identify *dependent* and *independent* variable(s). For some research designs, it is difficult or impossible to identify independent and dependent variables. This information is important to note. The choices for levels of measurement are:

   a. **nominal**: Individuals are assigned to a category such as male versus female versus nonbinary, or experimental group versus control group. If the design has one categorical variable, the number of levels of the variable is important information. Nominal variables can play two roles in experimental designs. In one role the frequency (number) of individuals in each category is the dependent variable. If the dependent variable is frequency counts, one of the chi-square tests is appropriate. On the other hand, if the independent variable is a nominal variable and the dependent variable is quantitative, a *t*-test or ANOVA would be appropriate. If a nominal variable cannot be identified, correlation or multiple regression are likely analysis strategies.

   b. **ordinal**: The classic definition of the ordinal level of measurement is that each individual is assigned a number indicating their relative rank (i.e., order). The numbers indicate relative positions but carry no quantitative information. This category does not appear very often in modern data analysis. However, there is a group of specialized tests that are appropriate for ordinal data such as the Mann-Whitney *U*-test, Wilcoxon rank-sum test, Kruskal-Wallis *H* test, and many others. See Siegel (1956) for a thorough discussion of rank-order tests. In modern statistical analysis the main value of these tests is for those occasions when a variable represents the ordinal level of measurement and the data do not meet the assumptions of the more powerful parametric tests such as the correlation coefficient, *t*-test, or analysis of variance.

   c. **quantitative or scale (SPSS term)**: These variables provide quantitative information about *how much* of some characteristic is present for each individual. Most psychological measures (e.g., IQ score, score on anxiety scale, GPA, height, heartrate, etc.) fit into this category of measurement. Another characteristic of quantitative measures is that plotting a frequency distribution results in a pattern that resembles a normal (bell-shaped) curve with most values being in the center, close to the mean, and fewer values being found further away from the mean in either direction. Computing a mean or average makes logical sense when the variable is quantitative. In sum, for most cases, identifying the nominal variables and quantitative variables in a study will point directly toward the correct analysis.

    d. **repeated measure**: A repeated measure occurs when the dependent variable is measured at different points in time. The number of times each person is measured, and whether one or more other independent variables are included in the design, are key determinants of the appropriate statistical test when a repeated measure is in the design.

4. Use the level of measurement to narrow down the list of potential tests that might be used. It is also helpful to categorize the design as requiring a test of **differences** versus a test of **relationship**.

    a. A **test of differences** examines whether there is difference for the dependent variable under different conditions. The only way that a test of differences makes sense is for the same variable to be compared under different conditions. The most common tests of differences involve comparing means of a quantitative variable under difference experimental conditions or for different groups. A test of differences requires that one or more nominal variables and at least one quantitative variable are part of the design. The only exception is repeated measures designs in which a dependent variable is compared to itself at different points in time and participants are tested or assessed more than once.

    b. A **test of relationship** involves the question of whether two or more different variables are related to or associated with each other. The most common test of relationship involves assessing the relationship between two quantitative variables with the Pearson correlation coefficient. Multiple regression involves one quantitative dependent variable and multiple quantitative independent variables. *QRST* also reviews several other important tests of relationship.

5. Make a selection based upon the specific characteristics of each statistical test. Be sure to consider whether the basic assumptions have been met or can be assumed to be met. If the basic assumptions of the more powerful parametric tests cannot be met, one of the nonparametric tests might be appropriate. This is a rare event because the Central Limit Theorem indicates that most quantitative variables will have a normal distribution. Furthermore, most parametric tests are quite **robust**, that is, results are not distorted by violations of the test's assumptions. When the variable does not have a normal or near-normal shape, it is possible that a **data transformation** can be used to address the problem. See below for a more detailed explanation.

6. Review your choice to ensure that it meets the requirements of the data analysis situation.

Choosing the appropriate test begins with knowledge of what statistical tests are available and the basic purpose of each test. Following is a list of tests typically studied in introductory statistics courses along with a description of each. Tests are grouped according to the level of measurement for which they are used and whether they are a test of differences or relationship. Chapter 8 provides more insight into the nature of the questions answered by each statistical test in the context of explaining how to use SPSS to conduct statistical analyses.

Tests of Relationship for Quantitative Data

Pearson Correlation

A correlation is a test of relationship between two *quantitative* variables. The correlation coefficient plays such a major role in data analysis that all of Chapter 3 was devoted to the topic. It is sometimes difficult to identify a clear DV or IV in a correlation study because a single correlation study cannot be used to infer causality. However, one variable in such a study might be labeled the independent variable for logical reasons. For example, if a study correlated the severity of bullying experienced by a child at age 8 years and depression at age 12, bullying might be labeled an independent variable because it precedes the measure of depression. However, a counterargument could be constructed (i.e., maybe children are already depressed before they are bullied) so it may be a challenge to label the variables in a correlational study. The Pearson correlation is a measure of the strength of linear relationship between *two* quantitative variables, so it is sometimes labeled *bivariate* correlation.

The basic design of a correlational study is that the researcher has collected data for two or more quantitative variables from most of the individuals participating in a study (some missing data is okay). The researcher is then interested in whether any pair of variables is related to each other. If the bivariate correlation between many pairs is computed, the results are typically presented in a correlation matrix where each cell of the matrix shows the correlation between a pair of variables. Thus, if the study has many quantitative variables, many bivariate correlations may be computed. These computations sometimes are the endpoint in a data analysis, but a matrix of bivariate correlations is often a precursor to more complex analyses such as multiple regression and factor/principal components analysis.

Bivariate Prediction

Prediction is based upon the Pearson correlation. It is a technique of using the correlation coefficient to predict one variable (e.g., college GPA) from another (e.g., ACT score). This would be part of the process of using tests in diagnosis or decision making. This topic is typically covered in tests and measurements courses. Bivariate prediction is not seen in empirical articles very often. However, it can be an important component of studies that assess the properties of diagnostic tests. Prediction was covered in Chapter 4 because it plays such an important role in tests and measures concepts.

Multiple Regression

Multiple regression is a general procedure in which a single quantitative dependent variable is predicted from two or more quantitative independent variables. As each new predictor or independent variable is added, its contribution can be assessed over and above the variables that have already been entered. The two specific multiple regression procedures are stepwise and hierarchical. These procedures are typically covered in advanced statistics courses, but knowledge of the basic terms will provide a head start.

a. **Stepwise multiple regression**: The order in which independent or predictor variables are entered into the regression equation is determined by the statistics with the variable having the strongest relationship to the dependent variable going first, followed by the remaining variable that adds the most to the prediction going next, and so on. The process continues as long as the contribution of the next variable is statistically significant. All the variables in the dataset are quantitative. One of the quantitative variables is designated by the researcher as the dependent variable. The remaining variables (two or more) are the independent variables. The researcher does not have a hypothesis or theory that guides the order in which variables are entered. There are two outcomes of this kind of analysis. First, there is a general measure (a multiple correlation coefficient) that indicates how well all the statistically significant IVs combined do at predicting the DV. Second, a relative ranking of how each individual variable does at predicting the DV is also obtained. A memory aid is that stepwise and statistics both begin with the letter *s*. Some research journals forbid publication of articles that use stepwise multiple regression. Instead, it is expected that a researcher has a theory or hypothesis specifying the order in which variables are entered into the regression equation. On the other hand, in my opinion, stepwise regression can be used as an effective screening technique when many independent variables have been measured in an exploratory study.

b. **Hierarchical multiple regression.** In this case, the researcher or hypothesis determines the order in which variables are entered into the multiple regression equation. This method is very useful because the order in which variables are entered can be used to statistically "control" for or eliminate the effects of one variable before the next variable is entered. For example, if a researcher wants to know the relationship between college GPA and optimism, they might measure GPA, ACT score, and optimism. Then they would perform a hierarchical regression entering ACT score first to control for the relationship of ability to GPA. Then they would enter optimism into the regression. The result would be an analysis that represents the relationship between optimism and GPA, controlling for ability. A memory aid is that hierarchical and hypothesis both begin with the letter *h*. Hierarchical multiple regression is common in research articles. I will mention a quirk of multiple regression that may seem puzzling when it is first encountered. Variables with two categories such as gender are often included in multiple regression analyses. The reason this works is a topic for advanced statistics courses. Chapter 8 explains how to conduct a simple hierarchical regression using SPSS.

Reliability

The bivariate correlation between a test and the same test administered at a different time is a measure of its **reliability**. Thus, reliability is a measure of the stability, consistency, or repeatability of a measure. One way to compute reliability is to compute the Pearson correlation between the first and second administrations of the same test (called test-retest reliability). Another way to compute reliability is to administer the test once and then combine the correlations among all the items that make up the measure to create a measure of internal consistency called **coefficient alpha** or Cronbach's alpha. This is easily computed with SPSS. Cronbach's alpha is easier to compute than test-retest reliability because it requires that the test be administered only once. Consequently, research articles are somewhat more likely to report Cronbach's alpha than test-retest reliability. Reliability is reported as a number between 0.0 and 1.00. The typical standards for reliability coefficients are: .70 and above for measures used in research, .80 and above for most other applications, and .90 and above for measures used in decision-making (e.g., IQ tests). When you read an article, the reliabilities of each quantitative measure should be reported. A measure with low reliability increases random variability and thus decreases statistical power compared to a measure with higher reliability. Thus, any research should begin with the most reliable measures of the constructs that are available.

Factor Analysis and Principal Components Analysis

These closely related procedures are used under the same circumstances but have different underlying assumptions and goals. Both procedures analyze bivariate correlations among a large set of variables to group related variables together. The most common application is to factor analyze or find the principal components of items that make up a measure of personality or a psychological construct. The procedure begins with a relatively large number of variables and the goal is to reduce these variables to subsets. No IVs, DVs, or grouping variables are involved. Most often the variables are the individual items of a test or measure. However, they can be any group of quantitative measures.

The analysis allows the researcher to group the items into factors or components that belong together because they appear to measure the same construct. For example, a factor analysis of an anxiety measure might result in two groups of items: one group relating to physical symptoms associated with anxiety and another related to cognitive symptoms. The key output is a table of *factor loadings* which are correlation coefficients indicating which variables relate to the same factor or component. In a research article, the items that belong together would be shown in groups along with the factor loadings. Factor analysis has no statistical significance tests associated with it. Together, factor analysis and coefficient alpha play key roles in the development of new psychological measures. Why is factor analysis important? It is a statistical technique frequently seen in research articles. If you are using a psychological measure in your own research, you should be aware of any factor analysis studies done with it. If the measure breaks down into two or more factors that have good reliability, the question that needs to be asked is whether each factor should be treated as a separate measure in your data analysis. See Thompson (2004) for a succinct and useful introduction to factor analysis. These factor analysis techniques are also called exploratory factor analysis (EFA).

There is another form of factor analysis called confirmatory factor analysis (CFA). The purpose of CFA is to determine how well a set of empirical data conform to a hypothesized factor structure for a set of variables. The key to interpreting a CFA is to look at the "fit indices," which measure how closely the empirical data conform to the hypothesized model. See Thompson (2004; pp. 127-130) and Byrne (2010; pp. 73-85) for descriptions of the various fit indices. One of the most popular fit indices is the root mean square error of approximation or RMSEA. RMSEA values of less than .05 indicate good fit of the model whereas values from .08 to .10 indicate mediocre fit. Poor fit is indicated by values above .10 (Byrne, 2010). Neither confirmatory nor exploratory factor analysis are covered in the typical introductory statistics course, but familiarity with these techniques will be helpful in comprehending research articles and easing the transition into advanced courses.

Tests of Differences for Quantitative Data

This group of tests involves testing whether the difference between two or more means is statistically significant. The key to this group of tests is that the dependent variable must be a quantitative measure, so it makes sense to compute a mean value. There will also be a nominal variable, in most cases, which divides subjects into groups. Introductory statistics classes cover all these tests and students would be expected to know them. An advanced statistics course might review all this material in a surprisingly short time, such as ten minutes or a single class period.

z-test for mean of a single-sample

This test is used when a sample mean is compared to a population mean when the *population standard deviation* is *known*. For instance, this test would be used when the research question is whether a sample from an institution is different from the population for a nationally administered test such as the SAT or ACT. In other words, the mean of a sample selected by the researcher is compared to the mean of the population, which is known from previous research, or available because the test is nationally administered. This test is much more likely to be used in program evaluation than to be found in a research article. Although classified as a test of differences, the z-test for a single sample, does not involve a nominal *variable* because it has only one group compared to the known value of the population.

t-test for a single sample

This procedure tests whether a sample mean differs from a population mean (just like the single-sample z-test) when the population standard deviation is *unknown* and must be estimated from the sample. This test has little practical use but may be seen in introductory statistics courses where it is a step toward more useful statistical tests. In the computer era, both the population mean and population standard deviation can be computed almost instantly, so it is extremely rare to know the population mean but not the population standard deviation. This test is taught in introductory statistics classes because it allows a gradual transition to more useful tests.

t-test for dependent means

A student who has taken an introductory statistics class would be expected to thoroughly understand this test and instantly recognize when it should be used. This test is used when the researcher wishes to know whether the means of a quantitative variable from two *dependent* samples are different. There are two ways to create dependent samples. By far the most common way is to administer the same measure at two different times. This is called a repeated measure design. Another way to produce dependent samples is when each participant in one group is matched with a participant in the other group on a variable for which the researcher would like to have both groups equalized. This technique has been replaced by more sophisticated multivariate methods taught in advanced courses and is only mentioned here for those reading older research articles. The repeated measure version of the dependent means t-test is commonly seen in empirical articles. The effect size (Cohen's d) is easily computed from the SPSS output as explained in Chapter 8.

t-test for independent means

This test is the highlight of many introductory statistics courses because it can be used to analyze data from a basic experimental study. The research question is whether means of two *independent* groups are different. There are *different participants* in each group and *no matching* is involved. The independent groups t-test is a very useful statistical test frequently seen in the empirical literature. In addition to a quantitative dependent variable, a t-test also has an independent or grouping variable with two levels such as diagnosis (anxious vs. not anxious) which is a measured variable. When a measured variable is used to classify subjects into groups, the researcher would be able to make a claim that the grouping variable is *associated* with the dependent variable, if the result is statistically significant. If it is possible to assign subjects to groups randomly, and the result is statistically significant, it means that the independent variable is manipulated, and the researcher has support for a causal claim that the manipulated variable causes the difference in the dependent variable. Reports of independent means t-test results should include the effect size. A convenient way to calculate it is to use this Internet site: http://www.cedu.niu.edu/~walker/calculators/effect.asp. This site computes Cohen's d and other effect size measures using the means, standard deviations, and sample sizes for the two groups as input. It is recommended that the output for Hedges' g be reported in articles, although it can be labeled as Cohen's d. Hedges' g is regarded as a less biased (more accurate) measure of effect size.

The researcher needs to have two variables to run an independent groups t-test. One variable is a nominal variable with two categories such as gender, diagnosis, or treatment versus control. This is called the **grouping variable** because it is used to place the participants into the two different groups. Alternately, the grouping variable can be called the independent variable. The grouping variable can be either measured or manipulated. The second variable needed for a t-test is a quantitative dependent variable. Thus, the researcher is asking whether the means of a quantitative dependent variable are different for two groups.

Assumptions for the *t*-test

The three varieties of the *t*-test make assumptions about the distribution of the data in the population, which is why they are called *parametric* tests. However, *t*-tests are also very *robust*, that is, resistant to violations of their assumptions. One important assumption is that the distribution of the data in the population has a normal shape. Although this assumption must be addressed in complex multivariate analyses, it is rarely assessed when the *t*-test is used because the sampling distribution will come to resemble a normal distribution with increasing sample size. A second assumption that applies to the independent groups *t*-test is that the *population* variances of the two groups are the same. SPSS output for an independent groups *t*-test provides a test of this assumption and a rarely needed alternative computation of the *t*-test that can be used if the assumption is violated.

A Review of Analysis of Variance

The analysis of variance (ANOVA) is an extremely versatile statistical procedure, frequently encountered in the empirical literature of psychology and other fields. It is rare to compute an analysis of variance by hand, because SPSS and other programs do the task much more quickly and accurately. This section provides information on how to decide that an ANOVA is the appropriate statistical analysis for a research problem. Introductory statistics classes vary widely in how much students are expected to learn about ANOVA. In my opinion, students who are reading *QRST* in preparation for an advanced statistics course at the undergraduate or graduate level should become thoroughly familiar with the vocabulary of ANOVA before they start their advanced class. It is also very likely that students doing their own research will need to use ANOVA. Chapter 8 discusses how to conduct an ANOVA using SPSS and interpret the output. An ANOVA is the appropriate statistical test when more than two means of a quantitative variable are included in the design. There are many kinds of ANOVA some of which are discussed in subsequent sections.

Assumptions in the Analysis of Variance

Most researchers do not concern themselves much with the assumptions that underlie the ANOVA because the procedure is robust, that is, it gives valid results even when its assumptions are violated. However, some combinations of conditions can invalidate results, so caution is prudent. The major statistical packages provide the option of testing for violations of assumptions. Use of these procedures is recommended when you are reporting the results of a study.

The assumptions of the analysis of variance are:
1.   The data for the dependent variable should be quantitative.
2.   The *population* distribution for each treatment condition should be normal.
3.   *Population* variances for all treatment conditions should be equal.
4.   For the repeated measures design, it is assumed that the covariance matrix has "compound symmetry" or "**sphericity**." This means that the covariances (similar to correlations) of the conditions are the same. SPSS reports a test for sphericity that can assess whether this assumption is violated.

Effect Size Measures in Analysis of Variance

Because a factor or independent variable in an ANOVA often has more than two levels, computing an effect size is an interesting problem. The typical approach is to use a proportion of variance explained measure, such as omega-squared (ω^2) or eta squared (η^2). The effect size conventions for eta squared are .01 for a small effect size; .06 for a medium effect size; and, .14 for a large effect size. These effect size measures are frequently seen in empirical articles and can be requested as a part of the SPSS output. Grissom and Kim (2005) suggest that when the focus is upon the difference between two particular means, a standardized effect size can be computed using S_P (the square root of the pooled variance estimate for the two means). This is easy to do and has the advantage of retaining the sign (direction) of the difference which can be very useful in meta-analyses, as opposed to proportion of variance explained measures which are squared so they cannot be negative. A convenient way to calculate a standardized effect size is to use this Internet site. This site computes Cohen's *d* and Hedges' *g*, and other effect size measures using the means, standard deviations, and sample sizes for the two groups as input. As noted, Hedges' *g* is typically reported but may be labeled as Cohen's *d*.

Analysis of Variance Vocabulary

F-ratio: The *F*-ratio is the final result of an analysis of variance. The *F*-ratio is compared to an *F*-distribution to determine whether the null hypothesis can be rejected. The rule is the same as for other tests of statistical significance: If the probability of obtaining a value of *F* is less than .05, the null hypothesis is rejected. One of the interesting characteristics of an analysis of variance is that one analysis may have any number of *F*-ratios, one for each main effect and interaction. The *F*-ratio is computed in such a way that the value of the ratio is close to 1.00 when the means are not different from each other and is greater than 1.00 when differences exist among the means. Analysis of variance analyzes variances (not means), so there is no directionality to *F*-ratios.

F-distribution: A family of *F*-distributions exists, with each distribution corresponding to the degrees of freedom in the numerator and denominator of the *F*-ratio. By locating the obtained value for the *F*-ratio on its respective *F*-distribution, it is possible to determine the probability of obtaining a value that large or larger. If the probability is less than .05, the null hypothesis is rejected. Software, such as SPSS, will report the exact probability of obtaining the result by chance. If the value is less than .05, the result is statistically significant.

Degrees of freedom: Degrees of freedom for an *F*-ratio are related to the number of treatment conditions and the number of participants in the treatment conditions. Each *F*-ratio has two values for degrees of freedom, one for the numerator and one for the denominator. The first *df* value (numerator) is small because it is based upon the number of treatment conditions and the second value (denominator) is much larger because it is determined by the number of participants in the groups or cells.

Factor: A factor is a single independent variable in an analysis of variance. The levels of a factor refer to the values that the factor has. If biological sex were a factor in a study, its levels could be male, female, and nonbinary. In a learning experiment, the researcher might be interested in the outcome for trials, where the effects of 3, 6, and 9 learning trials are compared. If the variable of interest was "college class" this independent or grouping variable would have four levels: first-year, sophomore, junior, and senior.

Main effect: A main effect is evaluated by computing an *F*-ratio that represents the effect of a single factor by itself, averaging scores across any other variables. Alternately, main effects can be seen as the outcome for a one-way ANOVA of one of the variables in a factorial design, ignoring all the other factors. There is one main effect for each factor in an analysis. Some texts call the means that are tested for differences, the marginal means, because they are in the margins of the table created when the design is diagrammed. For example, consider a two-factor study of learning in which students are taught under two conditions: group discussions (Cooperative) versus independent writing assignments (Independent). This is the first factor and could be labeled, type of learning experience. The second factor is biological sex, and has two groups or levels, males and females. Thus, the study has four conditions (male-cooperative; male-independent; female-cooperative; female-independent). The main effect of gender would result in an *F*-ratio that reflected the difference between males and females, ignoring the type of instruction. The main effect for type of instruction would result in an *F*-ratio that reflected only the difference between those in the cooperative versus independent conditions, ignoring the influence of gender. The third *F*-ratio in this design is the Gender X (by) Learning Experience interaction which is explained in the following section.

Interaction: In experiments with two or more factors, the experimenter is often interested in whether there is an interaction. An interaction is present when the effect of one factor depends upon or varies across levels of another factor. For example, consider the two-factor study of learning in which students are taught under two conditions: group discussions (Cooperative) versus independent writing assignments (Independent). This is the first factor and could be labeled, type of learning experience. The second factor is biological sex, and has two groups or levels, males and females. Thus, the study has four conditions (male-cooperative; male-independent; female-cooperative; female-independent). Assume that the dependent variable is an objective and essay test of knowledge gained in the course. An interaction would be present if the effect of learning method was different for the two sexes. One pattern that would meet this condition is that men and women perform the same under the Independent condition while they perform differently under the Cooperative condition. When the cell means of an interaction are graphed, the lines connecting means for one level of the first variable will not be parallel with lines connecting means at other levels of the same variable. Because the design described here has two factors, the analysis would result in three F-ratios, one each for the two main effects of Sex and Type of Learning Experience, and another F-ratio for the interaction of Sex and Type of Learning Experience. Interactions can consist of more than two factors, that is, it is possible to have three-way, four-way, or N-way interactions. However, most interactions described in the research literature are two-way interactions. When an analysis of variance is being interpreted, understanding the interaction(s) takes priority over the main effects.

Subsequent tests: When an analysis of variance factor has more than two levels, a significant F-ratio indicates that a difference, or differences, exist among the means. It does not indicate which mean or means differ from each other. When the overall F-ratio is significant, a subsequent test is typically used to clarify exactly where the difference or differences lie. One solution to this problem is to use an ordinary t-test or contrast to test pairs of means. When the F-ratio is significant, this is called a protected t-test. When the researcher has predicted the difference ahead of time, it is an *a priori* test. However, when there are many t-tests, or the researcher has not made predictions ahead of time, there is a concern that doing multiple t-tests may lead to a Type I error. That is, if ten t-tests are done at an alpha of .05, the chances of one being significant by chance is much higher than .05. Statisticians have developed many ways to deal with this issue, and there is abundant discussion concerning the best way. Specific tests used in this situation include the Newman-Kuels test, Tukey's HSD test, the Scheffé test, Fisher's LSD test, the Dunnett test, the Ryan procedure (the Ryan/Einot/Gabriel/Welsch range test, REGWQ), a Bonferroni correction, and the Benjamin-Hochberg Linear Step Up (LSU) procedure. These methods are more stringent than the methods for doing planned comparisons to provide better protection against Type I errors. When a factor has only two levels, no subsequent tests are needed. Howell (2010) suggests that the REGWQ or the Tukey procedure might be the best ways to test differences among a large number of means. Furthermore, Howell does not particularly like the Scheffé test, which was very popular in the past. Both tests (and many more) are available in SPSS. My personal favorite is the REGWQ test because the output for this test places the means in groups that are significantly different from each other while the means within the group are not significantly different from each other. If you are reading an empirical article that reports the results of an analysis of variance, you would interpret the results in four stages: first, figure out which F-ratios were statistically significant and, second, interpret the outcome of the subsequent tests (if any). Third, look at the actual means to learn exactly how the conditions or levels of the variable were different. Finally, evaluate the effect size for each variable.

Specific Analysis of Variance Procedures
Independent measures (one-way) analysis of variance

This test is similar to the t-test for independent means, except that more than two groups are involved. There is *one* independent (grouping) variable with more than two levels. For example, a researcher might examine the average amount of money gambled, the dependent variable (DV), as a function of type of gambler (Problem Gambler, Regular Gambler, or Occasional Gambler). The independent or grouping variable is Type of Gambler and the dependent variable is the amount of money gambled. The design would appear as shown below:

Problem Gamblers	Regular Gamblers	Occasional Gamblers
M = $556/hr	M = $98/hr	M = $158/hr

This design results in a single F-ratio. When it is statistically significant, some form of subsequent test is needed to clarify which means are different from each other.

Factorial analysis of variance

An ANOVA having *two or more* independent variables if a factorial design. Such designs are often designated like this: (number levels of 1st IV) X (number of levels of 2nd IV) X ... X (num. levels of last IV): e.g., a 2 X 2 X 3 ANOVA. For example, a researcher might look at the relationship of Gender/Sex (2 levels) and Type of Gambler (3 levels) on amount of money gambled. The resulting design would look like the one shown below. It would be called a 2 X 3 ANOVA or a 2 X

3 factorial. The two independent variables are gender and gambling style and the dependent variable is the amount of money gambled. A key component of interpreting factorial ANOVAs is the interactions among the variables. As noted earlier, an interaction occurs when differences for one factor of the design are different across levels of another factor. This design results in three F-ratios corresponding to two main effects and the one interaction.

	Problem Gamblers	Regular Gamblers	Occasional Gamblers
Males	M = $708/hr	M = $232/hr	M = $306/hr
Females	M = $481/hr	M = $77/hr	M = $98/hr

Figure 7-1 shows what the means for these hypothetical data look like when they are graphed. The graph indicates that the two independent variables do not have a significant interaction. Although men gamble more at each level of type of gambler, the magnitude of these differences remains stable across the three types of gambler. Furthermore, parallel lines indicate the absence of an interaction.

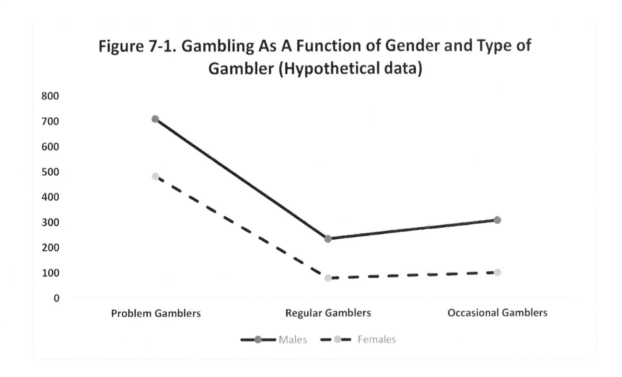

Figure 7-2 shows what these data might look like when there is an interaction. Here the lines are not parallel, and the pattern of differences varies across type of gambler. For Problem Gamblers and Occasional Gamblers, men gamble more money per hour than women. However, for Regular Gamblers, the opposite is true; women gamble more money per hour than males. Thus, in this hypothetical outcome, men and women gamblers behave differently as a function of Type of Gambler. Furthermore, the lines of the graph are not parallel which indicates that a statistically significant interaction is possible. Ultimately, the presence or absence of an interaction is indicated by the statistical significance of the corresponding F-ratio. However, most students find it easier to comprehend the concept of an interaction when it is illustrated graphically.

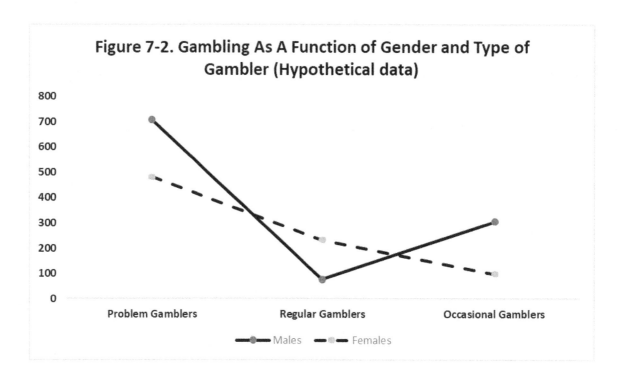

Figure 7-2. Gambling As A Function of Gender and Type of Gambler (Hypothetical data)

There are almost infinite possibilities of experimental designs that can be analyzed with ANOVA. However, there is a practical limitation on the number of factors that can be analyzed because each added factor increases the number of subjects needed. For instance, a three-way ANOVA could be created by adding a third factor such as income (Low, Medium, and High) to this hypothetical gambling study. The result would be 18 cells in the design. With a moderate 25 subjects per cell, the complete design would require 450 subjects. Not many researchers have the resources to run this many individuals through a study.

Repeated Measures and Mixed Designs
A repeated measures design involves measuring the same dependent variable at different points in time. For example, a researcher could obtain a sample of problem gamblers and measure the amount of money gambled per hour before and after they complete a treatment program. A design with a combination of repeated measures and grouping factors is called a mixed design.

Three Types of Analysis of Variance Covered in Advanced Courses and Seen in Research Articles

ANCOVA
Analysis of covariance. This is an analysis of variance that is performed after statistically adjusting (using bivariate or multiple regression) for one or more variables that are unwanted or that need to be controlled.

MANOVA
Multivariate analysis of variance. This is an analysis of variance performed upon two or more *dependent* variables. A significant result is usually followed by reports of exactly which of the dependent variables produced significant univariate (single-variable) results using a standard analysis of variance.

MANCOVA
Multivariate analysis of covariance is a combination of the ANCOVA and MANOVA procedures.

The Chi-square Tests: Goodness of Fit and Test for Independence

There are two chi-square tests: the chi-square test for goodness of fit and the chi-square test for independence. They are very important and often-seen statistical tests because the situations in which they are used are very common. For both tests the independent variable is a nominal variable (i.e., gender or political party) and the dependent variable is the frequency count for the categories of the nominal variable. The chi-square goodness of fit test answers the question of whether the frequency distribution for a single nominal variable is a good fit to an *expected* frequency distribution for the same nominal variable. The chi-square test for independence involves *two* nominal variables and the question is whether responses to one variable are related to or associated with responses to the other variable. Most authors classify the chi-square tests as nonparametric tests because they do not have restrictive assumptions about population distributions. However, some sources classify the chi-square tests as parametric (e.g., American Psychological Association, 2014).

A Test of Differences for Categorical (Nominal) Variables: Chi-square Test for Goodness of Fit

The chi-square test for goodness of fit examines how well a set of observed frequencies matches an expected or predicted distribution for those frequencies. One common hypothesis for a goodness of fit test is that frequencies should be equally distributed across categories. Another common use of a goodness of fit test is when past data (i.e., a survey conducted ten years ago) are compared to a recent administration of the same survey. Essentially, a chi-square goodness of fit test is needed when there is only one classification variable and the researcher has some logical, theoretical, or data-based hypothesis regarding how frequencies should be distributed across the categories.

For example, imagine that a student is taking a psychology class with 100 students and notices that there are more men than women and counts the number of males and females. The actual count would be the *observed* frequencies. If the student counted 70 females and 30 males, these would be the observed values. One approach to this problem would be to assume that the observed frequencies should be in proportion to the general population of 50% males and 50% females. This would translate into expected frequencies of 50 for males and 50 for females. A chi-square test would reveal whether the observed values are deviant enough from the expected values that it would be unlikely that the observed values came from a population of 50% males and 50% females. In this example the chi-square test was statistically significant meaning it is very unlikely that the observed data came from a population with a 50-50 split of males and females.

It is not necessary to assume expected values will be distributed equally among the categories of the nominal variable. National surveys indicate that about 77% of psychology majors are females. Thus, the observed count of 70 females and 30 males could be tested against expected values of 77 and 23. In this case the chi-square test was not statistically significant meaning that the observed data could have come from a population with a 77-23 split of males and females.

A Test of Relationship for Categorical (Nominal) Variables: Chi-square test for Independence

This test assesses whether two categorical (nominal) variables are independent of each other. The design of this test resembles the ANOVA because two independent variables are involved. However, the ANOVA has means or averages of a *quantitative* variable in the cells whereas the chi-square test has *frequency counts* in the cells. For example, adapting the above gambling example, we could ask whether males or females are more likely to be "problem gamblers." We could conduct a simple survey with two questions:

Are you a male or female? _____ Male _____ Female

Do you gamble too much? _____ Yes _____ No

These two variables could then be cross-tabulated to see if males and females tend to answer them differently. The result would be a 2 X 2 contingency table (or cross-tabulation) showing the frequency (number) of men and women who answered *yes* and *no* to the gambling question.

	Yes	No
Male	Observed frequency = 28	Observed frequency = 125
Female	Observed frequency = 13	Observed frequency = 136

It is extremely important to realize that the cells of a chi-square analysis contain *frequencies* (the observed count for each cell), whereas an ANOVA has *means* for a dependent variable inside each cell. The test is called a chi-square test for independence, and when the result is statistically significant, the conclusion is that the two variables are related, that is, they are dependent upon one another. In the above fictional data, it appears that males are more likely to report having gambling problems than females. Thus, the response to the questions about problem gambling depends upon the sex of the respondent.

The chi-square test for independence works best when each cell of the contingency table has a minimum frequency of five. If the cell frequencies are less than five, either Yate's correction or Fisher's Exact Test can be used to remedy the situation. Both options are available in SPSS. If the results of a chi-square test for independence are statistically significant it indicates the two nominal variables are related to each other. Then, the researcher would be interested in a measure of the strength of the relationship, that is, an effect size measure such as the phi coefficient or Cramer's phi. These measures convert the data in the contingency table into a measure similar to a correlation coefficient and indicate the strength of the relationship. These are also available as SPSS output.

Tests for Rank-Order (Ordinal) Data

Many decades ago, tests for rank-order data and nonparametric tests in general played a much more important role in statistical analysis. Today, they have become a rare sight in research articles. One reason is that the debate over classifying variables as being at the ordinal versus the interval level of measurement has lost the intensity that it had decades ago. For example, some might argue that college grade point average (GPA) represents measurement at the ordinal level. Nevertheless, it is treated as a quantitative measure in statistical analyses. This section provides a brief overview of these tests, so you will be familiar with them should they be encountered when reading empirical articles.

Table 7-1 shows the nonparametric ordinal tests along with their parametric equivalent.

Parametric Equivalent	Appropriate Rank-Order Test
dependent groups *t*-test	**Wilcoxon signed-rank test**
independent groups *t*-test	**Wilcoxon rank-sum; Mann-Whitney *U* test**
one-way ANOVA, independent groups	**Kruskal-Wallis *H* test**

Table 7-1. Common nonparametric ordinal tests and their parametric equivalents.

These tests are most likely to be encountered when reading an older empirical article. Alternately, these tests might be employed when the dataset has variables which violate assumptions of the appropriate parametric test. You may or may not be expected to be familiar with these tests in advanced statistics courses. See Siegel (1956) for a thorough review of nonparametric statistics.

Dealing with Violations of Assumptions

The parametric tests (correlation, multiple regression, the *t*-tests, and analysis of variance) make important assumptions about the distributions of the variables in the population. There are times when it is important to address these issues before data analysis is begun. This section describes strategies used to bring data into conformance with assumptions of parametric tests.

Data transformations

When data do not meet the assumptions of a parametric test, a common strategy is to perform a data transformation, which often corrects the problem, so the data now conform to the assumptions. A data transformation consists of performing some arithmetic operation on each individual score and then conducting the appropriate parametric analysis. Data transformations can correct non-normal distributions and heterogeneous variances, so the data meet the assumptions of parametric tests. Common examples are square root, logarithmic, and inverse transformations. For example, a square root data transformation can correct positive skewness because values that are furthest from the mean (e.g., the square root of 100 is 10) are brought closer to the mean than lower numbers such as 10 or 1. This strategy is used frequently. Table 7-2 shows several more common data transformations. Chapter 8 explains the procedures for requesting data transformations using SPSS.

Table 7-2. Useful Transformations and their Application

Transformation Type	Usefulness
Logarithmic	Heavy positive skew
Square-root	Moderate positive skew
Reciprocal	Negative skew
Arcsine	Binomial distribution

Levene's test for equality of variances.

This test is essential for understanding the independent groups t-test SPSS output. When it is significant, it means the population variances are different, that is, heterogeneous. This violates an assumption of the t-test. To address this a data transformation could be done, or the researcher could interpret the t-test results for "homogenous variances not assumed." In many cases, it is not necessary to address the issue because the results for both t-tests (homogeneous variances assumed and not assumed) are nearly identical.

Summary: Choosing the Correct Test

It takes hard work to develop the skill of choosing the correct test. The first step is to acquire the vocabulary of data analysis and research design. These terms are essential knowledge: independent and dependent variable; measured and manipulated variables; nominal (categorical), ordinal, and quantitative (scale) levels of measurement; grouping variable; normal distribution; and population versus sample. Then, a researcher should become familiar with as many of the available statistical tests as possible, beginning with those described in this chapter. It is not necessary to know how to compute each test or how to conduct the analysis with SPSS. Once the correct test is identified, numerous Internet tutorials and Chapter 8 of *QRST* can provide the necessary details.

When approaching a new problem, I like to focus on the level of measurement for each variable, paying close attention to quantitative variables. A more intuitive approach is to identify whether it makes sense to compute a mean. Quantitative variables are usually summarized with a mean so if a mean makes sense, a quantitative variable has been identified. When a sample mean is compared to a known population mean and the population *SD* is also known, a single-sample **z-test** is used. If the population *SD* is unknown or not given in the problem, a good question to ask is how many means (groups) are involved. If one or two means are involved, then one of the t-tests would be appropriate. If one mean is compared to a population mean, then a **single-sample t-test** (very rare) is used. If there are two means, the key question is whether a repeated measure or related samples (matching) is involved. If yes, the choice is a **dependent means t-test**. If no, the choice is an **independent means t-test**. If more than two means are involved, then an **ANOVA** is appropriate. Then, the number of independent variables determines the type of ANOVA. After an ANOVA is performed, the researcher needs to decide how he or she will determine which individual means are different from each other. The basic issue is whether the tests were **planned comparisons** versus **unplanned or *post hoc*** (Bonferroni, REGWQ, Scheffé, Tukey, and Neuman-Kuels are four common choices for unplanned tests).

If it is not possible or sensible to compute a mean, then one begins the search for an appropriate test by looking at the level of measurement and whether a test of differences or relationship is needed. If frequency counts of categorical variables are involved, one of the chi-square tests would work. If observed frequencies of a single variable are being compared to expected values, then a **chi-square goodness of fit** is appropriate. When the frequencies of one categorical variable are compared across levels of another categorical variable (i.e., there are two independent variables), then use a **chi-square test of independence**.

If two quantitative variables are involved in the problem, then one of the tests involving **correlation** is implicated. If the researcher wants to know the relationship between two different variables, both measured at the quantitative level, then a **Pearson correlation** is appropriate. Once a Pearson correlation coefficient has been computed, the researcher may wish to use it to predict scores on the dependent variable from scores on the predictor variable. This is called

bivariate prediction. If the researcher wants to know whether several independent variables can be used to predict one dependent variable, then a **multiple regression** should be performed. The type of multiple regression depends upon whether the researcher has a specific hypothesis, which suggests that the variables be entered in a specific order (**hierarchical regression**) or decides to let the statistics select the order of entry (**stepwise**). These two versions of multiple regression barely scratch the surface of what is possible with multiple regression procedures. A good reference book for multivariate statistics is Tabachnick and Fidell (2013).

Factor analysis, and **reliability** are special cases of tests of relationship. **Factor analysis** is useful when it is desirable to reduce many variables into a smaller group of variables (each consisting of separate clusters of the original variables). **Reliability** refers to a test's consistency or repeatability and is information that must be presented with psychological tests and in research articles.

The researcher also needs to consider whether the basic **assumptions** of the parametric statistics have been met when Pearson correlation, *t*-tests, or ANOVAs are used. When the assumptions are not met, a rank order transformation and the corresponding rank order test may be used. It is more common to use a **data transformation** and then run the appropriate parametric test.

Finally, if the data are ordinal to begin with (i.e., ranks) and the data are not normally distributed, then one of the tests for ordinal data could be chosen according to the type of question that needs to be answered.

To assess your understanding of choosing the appropriate statistical test, various research scenarios are described on the next page and your task is to choose the appropriate analysis for each scenario. An answer key is provided on the page that follows the exercise.

Self-Assessment Quiz for Chapter 7

For each of the following examples, select the appropriate method of statistical analysis and briefly note the reasons behind your choice. Both your choice and the explanation will be graded (10 points each). A series of bullet points is the most efficient way to explain your choice.

1. A researcher is interested in whether male basketball players are taller than the typical male so she gathers a random sample of 100 male college basketball players and measures the height of each and compares it to the population value for males of 70 inches. The researcher was unable to find the standard deviation of the population.

   Single Sample t-test
   - *1 DV*
   - *Pop SD Unknown*

2. This time the researcher wanted to know whether the SAT scores of basketball players were different from the population mean of 500 (with a known population standard deviation of 100). She took a random sample of 250 college basketball players, determined the SAT score of each and compared the average of her sample to the population parameters.

   Single Sample Z-test
   - *1 DV*
   - *Pop SD is known*

3. (a) A researcher was interested in whether a new drug was effective for relieving pain. A test was conducted by randomly assigning 30 participants to receive the active drug and 30 participants to receive a placebo. The researcher then measured the amount of time that each participant could keep their non-preferred hand submerged in a bowl of ice water.

   Dependent sample t-test
   - *1 DV*
   - *Matching subjects*
   - *Comparing two means*

   (b) If the researcher in this example was concerned about violations of the assumptions for the test, name one strategy could she use instead of a parametric test?

4. A researcher wanted to test whether greater optimism might be related to scores on a statistics final exam. A sample of 100 students from various statistics courses were given a test of optimism prior to taking their regularly scheduled statistics final. What statistical analysis should be performed?

5. Our researcher from Example 3 obtained positive results but then was asked what the optimum dose for the new medication was and whether males and females differed in their response to the new drug. A group of 120 volunteer women were randomly assigned to receive doses of 0 mg., 5 mg., 10 mg., and 15 mg., and 120 mg. volunteer men were also randomly assigned to receive the same doses. The researcher then measured the time that each participant could keep their non-preferred hand submerged in a bowl of ice water.

6. A researcher was interested in whether "Hooked on Phonics" was better than taking a child to the library as a means of improving reading skills over the summer. The researcher obtained a sample of 100 fourth-grade girls

and 100 fourth-grade boys and randomly assigned them to one of two groups. The first group followed the "Hooked on Phonics" program under supervision of their parents. The second group was taken to the public library by their parents to check out and read at least two books each week. The program began on June 1 and ended on August 30. On September 1, all 200 students were given the same standardized test of reading achievement.

7. A Psychologist was interested in learning about depression in college students. She obtained a random sample of 500 college students from several colleges and asked them to complete a packet consisting of a depression scale, a measure of satisfaction with social relationships, a measure of optimism, a measure of daily college life hassles, and a measure of three different coping styles for dealing with negative events. The researcher is interested in whether depression can be predicted from scores on the other six instruments.

8. The researcher in Problems 3 and 5 hears reports that the new pain medication has a critical side effect; it may cause drowsiness. Consequently, she decides to run a simple experiment to determine if the new drug has any effect on reaction times. One randomly assigned group is given a 10 mg. dose and a second group is given a placebo and both groups are then tested for reaction times to an emergency in a simulated driving test. A test indicates that the two groups come from populations with different variances. Suggest an appropriate strategy for dealing with this situation.

9. After doing the study described in Problem 8, our researcher begins to suspect that there may be a gender difference in the way that men and women respond to the new drug. She suspects that the proportion of males who are "responders" is greater than the proportion of females who are "responders." To test this hypothesis she reviews all her previous data using the 10 mg. dose and classifies all the participants into two categories: gender (male and female) and whether or not they were "responders" (yes or no) to the medication. What is the best method of statistical analysis?

10. The researcher continues to be interested in how men and women respond to the "ice water" test and she decides to conduct another study. This time she obtains 10 male and 10 female volunteers and simply has each individual place their hand in the ice water for as long as they can. One look at the raw data (time of keeping hand in ice water) indicates that many outliers are present. How should these data be analyzed?

11. A researcher is interested in whether students who have taken statistics class are better problem solvers than those who have not taken a statistics class. He obtains a sample of 30 students who are about to take a statistics class and asks them to take the XYZ Problem Solving Test. At the end of the semester after the course has been completed, the same group of students retake the XYZ Problem Solving Test. What is the appropriate statistical test?

12. A researcher wants to know the relationship between ACT scores and cumulative GPA at the end of the first year of college. He obtains data from a random sample of 200 first-year students at a local university.

13. A researcher is developing a measure of organizational leadership processes. He develops a group of 100 items and administers them via a confidential survey to 450 volunteers. The first question the researcher asks is whether there are groups of items that tend to measure the same characteristic of an organization. What is the best statistical method of answering this question?

14. A researcher is interested in comparing academic motivation for a randomly selected sample of students attending private college institutions and a random sample of students attending public, state funded colleges. What statistical analysis would be appropriate?

15. A researcher is interested in the effects of a GRE preparation course so he administers a short version of the GRE to a group of seniors who then participate in the prep course. The practice GRE is then readministered to the same group. What statistical test would be appropriate in this case? Why?

16. A researcher is interested in the effectiveness of various ways of preparing for the GRE preparation course so he identifies a group of 60 seniors who are randomly assigned to participate in a prep course, practice for the GRE on their own, or solve Sudoku problems for two hours a night. After three weeks the practice GRE is then administered to these students. What statistical test would be appropriate in this case? Why?

Answers to Problems

1. Single-sample *t*-test
2. Single-sample *z*-test
3. (a) independent groups *t*-test; (b) data transformation or use *t*-test results for heterogeneous variances
4. Correlation coefficient (Pearson)
5. 2 X 5 factorial ANOVA
6. 2 X 2 factorial ANOVA
7. Stepwise multiple regression
8. Perform a data transformation and then an independent groups *t*-test; use results for heterogeneous variances
9. 2 X 2 chi-square test of independence
10. Data transformation followed by independent groups *t*-test
11. A dependent means (repeated measure) *t*-test
12. Pearson correlation coefficient
13. Factor analysis or principal components analysis
14. Independent groups *t*-test
15. A dependent means *t*-test
16. One-way ANOVA

Chapter 8: Using SPSS and Describing Results

IBM SPSS Statistics software (SPSS) is the Windows version of the Statistical Package for the Social Sciences. A new version appears annually, but changes are minor from year to year. It is a useful, popular, and easy-to-use software package for performing statistical analyses. Becoming familiar with SPSS may be an important step in your professional or educational advancement. The purpose of this chapter is to explain the basics of using the program beginning with data entry and computing the correlation between two variables and continuing with *t*-tests, ANOVAs, chi-square, and multiple regression.

This chapter also shows examples of reporting results in research articles or student papers because many readers will be producing research reports as part of their course experience. For those who have more complex goals such as analyzing data for potential publication, I recommend finding a recent issue of the journal to which the work will be submitted and modeling the presentation of results based upon recent articles that report similar analyses. There are several basic rules about presenting results following the style rules of the American Psychological Association (2010) that all social science researchers need to know. They are listed below.

- Statistical symbols should be in *italics*. This includes *df, F, M, N, n, r, SD, t, z*, Cohen's effect size *d*, and others.
- The Greek symbol for chi is set in regular face type, e.g., χ^2.
- The equal sign (=) has a single space before and after it.
- The word, *data*, is treated as a plural word in APA style.
- Note that the preferred typeface for APA manuscripts is Times New Roman set in 12-point size.
- Tables are typically done in a *sans serif* type (i.e., Calibri, Arial).
- Refer to the *APA Publication Manual* (American Psychological Association, 2010) for additional details.
- For quick guidance on formatting an article see the sample papers (pp. 41-59) in the *APA Publication Manual*.

Using *SPSS* to Compute a Correlation

This section has two purposes. The first is to explain how to enter data into SPSS. The second is to review the basics of computing, interpreting, and reporting a correlation coefficient using SPSS.

A Review of Correlation

A correlation coefficient measures the degree of linear relationship between two *quantitative* variables. Generally, correlations are computed between two *different* variables that have been measured for the same group of people. Each person or case in the sample provides a score on each of the two variables. For example, a researcher might be interested in the relationship between college GPA and the average number of hours the student studies. Hopefully, the result would be a positive correlation with higher GPAs associated with more hours of study. Hypothetical data for such a study are shown in Table 8-1.

Table 8-1. Sample Dataset for Computing a Correlation Coefficient

Participant	College GPA	Weekly Study Hrs
Participant #01	1.8	15
Participant #02	3.9	38
Participant #03	2.1	10
Participant #04	2.8	24
Participant #05	3.3	36
Participant #06	3.1	15
Participant #07	4.0	45
Participant #08	3.4	28
Participant #09	3.3	35
Participant #10	2.2	10
Participant #11	2.5	6

There are eleven participants, each having a score on both the GPA variable and the Weekly Study Hours variable. SPSS also uses the spreadsheet format shown here and automatically numbers each row. Each *row* of the spreadsheet is called a *CASE* which is one of the participants in the study. Each *column* of the spreadsheet stores numerical values for each variable for which data have been collected, such as GPA and Weekly Study Hours, as shown here, or other information relevant to the study. Thus, each column has a different variable with a value for each person or case in the study. Complex studies may have thousands of participants and hundreds of variables. If data are missing, a dot appears in the cell instead of a number. In most studies, a "CASE" is an individual participant. However, it is possible to define a "CASE" as something other than a human participant. For example, each "CASE" in a study could be a different elementary school about which researchers have gathered information.

Starting Up SPSS

To make it easier to follow command sequences, italicized **bold font** indicates SPSS commands in this chapter. SPSS is usually part of the general network available in computer labs and residence halls of most college campuses and many businesses. To activate SPSS, sign-on to the network with your username and password. Then click the **Start** icon in the lower left-hand corner of the screen followed by ***Network Programs → SPSS for Windows → SPSS for Windows***. If SPSS is not found on the "Network Programs" group, it may be installed as a "local program" in which case the proper sequence is **Start > Programs → Local Programs → SPSS**. If you are using Windows 10, go to the Start button on the lower left of the home screen and click ***All apps*** and look for ***IBM SPSS***. Another possibility is that a shortcut already exists on the desktop, in which case double-clicking it will open the SPSS program. Do not spend a long time trying to open the SPSS program. If you have trouble, call or visit your institution's Helpdesk, search for information on your local network, contact your instructor, or ask for help from your peers.

The SPSS Program

After clicking the SPSS icon, there is a short delay, after which the SPSS program appears. *IBM SPSS Statistics 26* begins with two windows. The top window offers several options which may be useful eventually, but the easiest thing to do is close the top window, giving access to the main program. Thanks to a user-friendly interface, it is possible to do almost anything from simple descriptive statistics to complex multivariate analyses with a few mouse clicks. The program will not execute a procedure until the researcher enters all the necessary information. Although it can be frustrating when doing complex procedures, it saves time because the immediate feedback increases efficiency.

Data Input for SPSS

SPSS appears on the screen looking like most other Windows programs. See Figure 8-1 for an example of an SPSS data input widow and the input screen for computing a correlation. Two tabs are available in the lower left corner: **Data View** and **Variable View**. When SPSS first comes up, it is ready to accept new data. First, look at the menu options across the top of the screen:

<u>F</u>ile <u>E</u>dit <u>V</u>iew <u>D</u>ata <u>T</u>ransform <u>A</u>nalyze Direct <u>M</u>arketing <u>G</u>raphs <u>U</u>tilities Add <u>on</u> <u>W</u>indow <u>H</u>elp

These menu options are the entry points for accessing the features of the SPSS program. Clicking one of these options opens a menu of related options and input windows, which allows the user to specify variables to include in analyses.

However, before analyses can be conducted, data must be available. To begin the process of a computing a correlation, click on the **Variable View** tab at the bottom left, then enter information about each variable. Type a short name for the first variable that will be easy to remember. For example, the first variable in the above example could be called **ColGPA**, a name that gives a good indication of the nature of the variable (college GPA). To provide a short label for each variable in the study, simply type its name in the **Name** column. The next column labeled **Type** allows the researcher to designate a variable type using the drop-down menu. "Numeric" is the most common choice. The **Width** and **Decimals** columns determine how the data are displayed. It is also useful to have more information about the variable and this is done by clicking on the cell in the **Label** column corresponding to the variable. This allows you to add an extended label, such as **College GPA for 2019**. You can also add **value labels** using the cell in the **Values** column. Value labels allow you to label the *values* of a nominal or categorical variable. For example, most studies have a variable called Sex or Gender that can take on two or more values, 1 = Female; 2 = Male; 3 = nonbinary; 4 = prefer not to answer, etc. The **Values** column allows you to have these labels attached to all the output from statistical analyses, which simplifies interpretation and reporting. Entering value labels also means you don't need to remember how the variable was coded (i.e., whether males were coded 1 or 2) when you view the output. After entering information for the first variable, go to the next row and repeat the process for the second variable. Continue defining variables until all the variables have been defined.

The second to last column on the Variable View screen provides a drop-down list of variable types that can be chosen for each variable. The choices are: nominal, ordinal, and scale. "Scale" corresponds to quantitative. Occasionally, a variable fails to show up in a list as expected. When this happens, it is helpful to check this column to ensure that the variable has been correctly classified. Similarly, the column labeled "Type" can result in the same problem. For example, if a variable has the words "male" or "female" entered in each cell instead of a numerical code, it will be labeled a "string" variable. In this case it would need to be recoded from a string variable to a numeric variable to be useable in SPSS.

Once the variables have been defined, the data can be entered in the spreadsheet. (These tasks can be done in the opposite order, as well.) This requires working with the **Data View** tab. To begin, make sure the cursor is flashing at the top of the spreadsheet window and that the upper left cell of the spreadsheet is highlighted. To highlight a cell, use the mouse to move the cross to the desired cell of the spreadsheet and click the left mouse button. The arrow keys also work well to navigate around the spreadsheet. Begin entering data by typing the first piece of data. In the above example, the first entry would be **1.8**. This number will appear at the top of the spreadsheet. Hit **<ENTER>** to move the data into the correct cell. Notice that after hitting **<ENTER>** the second cell in the first column is now highlighted. The next piece of data (**3.9**) can be entered using the same procedure. Thus, data are automatically entered vertically. Continue until all the data for the first column have been entered. After entering all the data for the first column, use the mouse or arrow keys to highlight the first cell in the second column and begin entering the second column of data using the same technique. If a piece of data is missing (e.g., the participant did not answer one or more of the questions on a survey), simply hit **<ENTER>** when the input cell at the top of the spreadsheet is empty. This will cause a dot to appear in the spreadsheet cell which is interpreted by SPSS as missing data. SPSS has very flexible options for handling missing data. Usually, the default or standard option is the best.

In larger studies with numerous variables, it may be more convenient to go across or horizontally, entering all the data for the first participant followed by all the data for the second participant, continuing until all data have been entered. To do this, it will be necessary to make more frequent use of the mouse and/or the arrow keys to highlight the next cell going across each row. When data for a large study are being entered, it is best to work with a partner. One person can read the data and the other can type, greatly increasing speed and accuracy.

Advanced Data Entry and File Handling

SPSS is capable of reading files from several formats such as Excel spreadsheets which might be the format for the raw data from various devices and survey management programs. Go to **File → Open → Data** and use the drop-down menu to select the appropriate file type. When importing data in this manner, it is important to check for "string" variables and confirm that the variable type (nominal, ordinal, or scale) is correct.

Computing the Pearson Correlation

After entering data, the next step is to order the program to compute the correlation coefficient. Use the mouse to go to the top of the screen and click on the following sequence: **Analyze → Correlate → Bivariate**. This will open another input window. Figure 8-1 shows an example of the correlation input window. [All screenshots of IBM® SPSS® Statistics software (SPSS) input windows are courtesy of International Business Machines Corporation, © International Business Machines Corporation.]

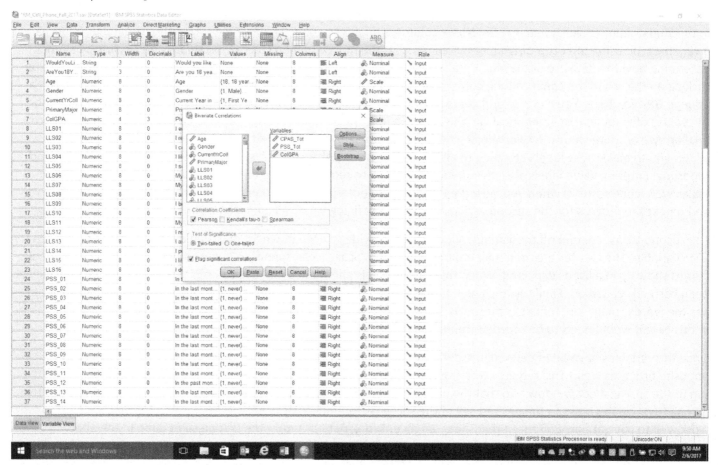

Figure 8-1. Example variable view window and correlation input window for *IBM SPSS Statistics 26*.

The smaller window, labeled Bivariate Correlations, is where the information for computing the correlation is entered. Inside this window, you will see two boxes with the one on the left containing the complete list of variables for the study. The variables may appear in alphabetical order. However, it can be more convenient to display the variables in the same order as they appear on the spreadsheet or input window. The display order can be changed by clicking **Edit →** **Options → General** tab. Then change "Alphabetical" to "File" by clicking the empty circle next to "File" under "Display Order for Variable Lists." I also prefer to display "names" of variables instead of the labels because the labels are so long. After making the desired changes, go back to the Bivariate Correlations input window. The box on the right will be empty. Between the boxes is a right-pointing arrow. The sequence for computing a correlation is to highlight variables from the list on the left and then use the mouse to click the right-pointing arrow. This will cause each highlighted variable to jump to the box on the right. Each variable in the box on the right will be included in the correlation matrix computed by SPSS. Other Windows conventions such as drag and drop can be used to move variables over. Thus, to compute the correlation between ColGPA and StudyHrs, move both variables over to the box on the right. A variable can be removed from the box on the right by highlighting it and clicking the arrow in the middle, which will now face in the opposite direction. Once the desired variables are in the right-hand box, the **OK** button may be clicked which will cause the correlations to be computed and appear in an Output window. However, a couple of additional options are worth considering.

First, is extremely helpful to click the **Options** button, which appears on the right side of the input window. This will cause another input window to appear. Generally, all options can be left on their default settings. However, one option allows you to print means and standard deviations for each variable by just clicking the box. This is worth doing. The other options should be left alone unless you have a specific reason for changing one. At this point, click the **Continue** button to close this box and move on with your task. If confidence intervals for the correlations are desired, one method for getting them is to click the **Bootstrap...** button, click the box next to **Perform Bootstrapping**, leave the other options at the default values, and then click **Continue**. The output will then include confidence intervals that can be reported along with the correlation coefficient. The final step is to click the **OK** button.

After a short delay, an Output window will appear with the results of your analysis. The information in the output file can be viewed or saved to a file using standard Windows conventions. Tables can be copied and pasted into word processing files. Additional analyses can be performed, and their results will be appended to the end of the current output window so the results of a complex series of analyses can be contained in one output window. Be sure to give this file a name that will remind you of its contents. I like to include the date the file was created as part of the file name. Results for a sample size of N = 474 are shown in Tables 8-2a and 8-2b.

Table 8-2a shows means, standard deviations, and the sample size for the two correlated variables in the column labeled **Statistic**. The other columns can be ignored.

Table 8-2a Descriptive Statistics

Descriptive Statistics

| | | Statistic | Bootstrap[a] | | | |
| | | | | | 95% Confidence Interval | |
		Statistic	Bias	Std. Error	Lower	Upper
Please enter your cumulative GPA in the box	Mean	3.3300	.0005	.0204	3.2881	3.3709
	Std. Deviation	.44810	-.00097	.01598	.41771	.47987
	N	474	0	0	474	474
WielkLLSTot	Mean	61.1203	.0132	.4841	60.1604	62.0476
	Std. Deviation	10.21649	-.01250	.49475	9.32718	11.25446
	N	474	0	0	474	474

a. Unless otherwise noted, bootstrap results are based on 1000 bootstrap samples

To interpret the correlation output, look at the table labeled Correlations (8-2b).

Table 8-2b, Correlation Output for Bootstrapped Correlation

Correlations

			Please enter your cumulative GPA in the box	WielkLLSTot
Please enter your cumulative GPA in the box	Pearson Correlation		1	.238**
	Sig. (2-tailed)			.000
	N		474	474
	Bootstrap[c]	Bias	0	.002
		Std. Error	0	.052
		95% Confidence Interval	Lower	1	.139
			Upper	1	.339
WielkLLSTot	Pearson Correlation		.238**	1
	Sig. (2-tailed)		.000	
	N		474	474
	Bootstrap[c]	Bias	.002	0
		Std. Error	.052	0
		95% Confidence Interval	Lower	.139	1
			Upper	.339	1

**. Correlation is significant at the 0.01 level (2-tailed).

c. Unless otherwise noted, bootstrap results are based on 1000 bootstrap samples

This is a correlation matrix with seven values for each correlation. The top row shows Pearson correlation coefficient, which will range from -1.00 to +1.00. The further away the correlation is from zero, the stronger the relationship. The first correlation shown is between ColGPA and ColGPA, which results in a value of 1. The next correlation in the row is between ColGPA and the Lifelong Learning Scale (Wielkiewicz & Meuwissen, 2014). In this study the correlation was .238, which is between a medium and small effect size. The next row [Sig. (2-tailed)] shows the probability. Remember, you are looking for probabilities *less than* .05 in order to reject the null hypothesis and conclude that the correlation differs significantly from zero. The first box is blank because the correlation between ColGPA and ColGPA is not relevant. With a two-tailed significance of .000, the correlation coefficient between ColGPA and the Lifelong Learning Scale is statistically significant. The third row is the sample size, $N = 474$. With only two variables, the sample size is constant. However, when more than two variables are included, the sample size may vary due to missing data. Note that asterisks also show that the correlation is statistically significant. Asterisks indicate statistical significance in tables summarizing many results with a key shown at the bottom of the table. When the correlation coefficient cannot be computed, it is represented as a dot. The diagonal of the matrix shows the correlation of each variable with itself which is always 1 and the correlations below the diagonal will be a mirror image of the correlations above the diagonal. The **bootstrapping** procedure resulted in a 95% confidence interval for the correlation of .139 to .339. The confidence interval does not include zero, which is consistent with the low probability.

Using the calculator at this website, I found the confidence interval for $r = .238$, $N = 474$, which was 95% CI [.151, .321]. This indicates that there is a 95% chance that the true value of the population correlation is between .151 and .321. With the large sample size, both methods result in a narrow confidence interval. The small difference between the bootstrap results and the calculated results is that the bootstrap method provides a more precise estimate that is not affected by violations of the normality assumption. The **_Bootstrap..._** option, if it is available in the version of SPSS you are using, is somewhat more convenient. A more detailed tutorial on this method can be found here.

Another important thing to do when computing a correlation is to look at the scatter diagram. To produce a scatterplot, click **Graphs → Legacy Dialogs → Scatter/Dot**. Use the same technique as before to transfer variables to the x-axis and y-axis boxes. Then click **OK** and the graph will appear in the output file. To insert the plot in another document, right-click your mouse, click copy, and paste it into your document. Viewing the scatterplot will help you identify nonlinear relationships and other issues with the data.

Some Rules Can be Broken

The main application of the correlation coefficient is to determine the strength of the linear relationship between two *quantitative* variables, but there's an important exception. If a dataset contains a nominal (categorical) variable with two categories, such as gender, you might see that variable included in a correlation matrix. This is perfectly legitimate, and the information contained in the correlation is the same as would be provided by conducting an independent groups *t*-test. This fact is often used in explanations of the **General Linear Model,** which is an overarching model that puts all statistical analyses under one umbrella. However, if you are taking an introductory statistics course, the rule that correlation can be used only for two *quantitative* measures (e.g., GPA and ACT score) typically cannot be broken.

Describing Your Results

After the analysis is complete, it may be necessary to include the results in a paper. The example below describes the results of this correlation as they might appear in a paper or article. The 95% confidence interval is optional and probably omitted by most authors. However, its inclusion reminds the reader of the variability associated with a sample correlation coefficient. In the future, confidence intervals may become required elements of most analyses.

> The correlation between college GPA ($M = 3.33$; $SD = .45$) and the Lifelong Learning Scale ($M = 61.12$; $SD = 10.21$) was statistically significant, $r = .238$, $N = 474$, $p = .000$, 95% CI [.151, .321]. In general, higher GPAs were associated with higher scores on the Lifelong Learning Scale.

I chose to present the calculated values, instead of the bootstrapped values, for the confidence interval because they represent the more traditional approach. Confidence intervals for the correlation coefficient are typically not presented in published research, so the rules for how to present them are not yet standardized. If a study has many correlation coefficients, they are often presented in a correlation matrix, which shows all the correlations among a group of variables. A correlation matrix looks like a typical spreadsheet with the first column listing all the variables. Each variable is numbered so only variable numbers are shown across the top row. The diagonal will show the correlations of each variable with itself, which will all be equal to 1.00. Because the diagonal correlations *must* be equal to 1.00, this information is sometimes omitted in favor of showing the reliability of each variable. Also, the correlations above and below the diagonal are redundant. Thus, the areas above and below the diagonal can be used to show correlations for different groups, such as college students versus employed adults. If a researcher is planning to publish a study for which a correlation matrix will be presented, it may be helpful to look at the journal to which a submission is planned for examples.

The *t*-test for Independent Groups with SPSS

The *t*-test is used for testing differences between two means. The *same dependent variable* must be measured in different groups, at different times, or in comparison to a known population mean. Comparing a sample mean to a known population mean is an unusual test that appears in some statistics books as a transitional step in learning about the *t*-test. The more common applications of the *t*-test are testing the difference between independent groups or testing the difference between dependent or related groups.

A *t*-test for independent groups is used when the same variable has been measured in two independent groups, and the researcher wants to know whether the difference between group means is statistically significant. "Independent groups" means that the groups have different people in them and that the people in the different groups have not been matched or paired in any way. A *t*-test for related samples or *t*-test for dependent means is the appropriate test when the *same* people have been measured under two different conditions or at two different times. Alternately, matched pairs can create dependent groups.

When to use the *t*-test For Independent Groups

A *t*-test for independent groups compares the difference between means of two groups on the same dependent variable. Groups may be formed in two ways. First, a preexisting characteristic may be used to divide participants into groups. For example, the researcher may wish to compare college GPAs of men and women. In this case, the **grouping variable** is biological sex and the two groups would consist of men versus women. Other preexisting characteristics that could be used as grouping variables include age (under 21 years vs. 21 years and older), athlete (plays collegiate varsity sport vs. does not play), type of student (undergraduate vs. graduate student), type of faculty member (tenured vs. nontenured), married vs. single, or any other variable for which it makes sense to have two categories. Another way to form groups is to randomly assign participants to one of two experimental conditions such as a group that listens to music versus a group that experiences a control condition. Regardless of how the groups are determined, one of the variables in the SPSS data file must contain the information needed to divide participants into the appropriate groups and a second variable must contain the scores on the dependent measure.

Like all other statistical tests using SPSS, the process begins with data. Consider the fictional data on college GPA and weekly hours of studying used previously. Let's add information about the biological sex of each participant, using a binary classification. This requires a numerical code. For this example, let a "1" designate a female and a "2" designate a male. With the new variable added, the data would look like the spreadsheet shown below.

Participant	GPA	Study Hrs	Biological Sex
Participant #01	1.8	15	2
Participant #02	3.9	38	1
Participant #03	2.1	10	2
Participant #04	2.8	24	1
Participant #05	3.3	36	.
Participant #06	3.1	15	2
Participant #07	4.0	45	1
Participant #08	3.4	28	1
Participant #09	3.3	35	1
Participant #10	2.2	10	2
Participant #11	2.5	6	2

With this information added to the file, two methods of dividing participants into groups can be illustrated. Note that Participant #05 has a single dot in the column for biological sex. This indicates missing data. This is a common occurrence, especially in survey data, and SPSS has flexible options for handling this situation. Begin the analysis by entering the new data for biological sex. Use the arrow keys or mouse to move to the empty third column on the spreadsheet. Use the same technique as before to enter the new data. When data are missing (such as Participant #5 in this example), hit the <ENTER> key when there is no data in the top line (you will need to <DELETE> the previous data from the top) and a single dot will appear in the variable column. Once the data are entered, click the **Variable View** tab and type in the name of the variable, "BioSex." Then go to "value" column and type a "1" in the box. For "Value Label," type "Female." Then click on **ADD**. Repeat the sequence, typing "2" and "male" in the appropriate boxes. Then click **ADD** again. Finally, click **CONTINUE → OK** and you will be back to the main SPSS menu.

To request the *t*-test, click **Analyze → Compare Means → Independent-Samples T Test**. Use the right-pointing arrow to transfer ColGPA to the "Test Variable(s)" box. Then highlight BioSex in the left box and click the bottom arrow (pointing right) to transfer sex to the "Grouping Variable" box. Then click Define Groups. Type "1" in the Group 1 box and type "2" in the Group 2 box. This feature allows the researcher to choose the two levels of the variable that will be compared. For example, if the gender question included a third option that stated, "prefer not to respond," it could be excluded from the analysis. Then click **Continue**. Click **Options** and you will see the confidence interval, or the method of handling missing data can be changed. Since the default options are fine, click **Continue → OK** and results will appear in the output window as shown in Tables 8-3a and 8-3b. Note that more subjects were included in this analysis than are shown in the example.

Table 8-3a. Group Statistics for Independent Groups *t*-test

	BioSex	N	Mean	Std. Deviation	Std. Error Mean
ColGPA	male	10	2.8000	.72877	.23046
	female	11	2.8545	.72161	.21757

Table 8-3b. Independent Samples Test

		Levene's Test for Equality of Variances		t-test for Equality of Means					95% Confidence Interval of the Difference	
		F	Sig.	T	df	Sig. (2-tailed)	Mean Diff	Std. Error Diff	Lower	Upper
ColGPA	Equal variances assumed	.171	.683	-.172	19	.865	-.05455	.31678	-.71758	.60849
	Equal variances not assumed			-.172	18.772	.865	-.05455	.31694	-.71845	.60936

The output begins with Table 8-3a, the means and standard deviations for the two variables, which is key information that will need to be included in the research report. Table 8-3b shows the outcome of the *t*-test. "Levene's Test for Equality of Variances" is a test of the homogeneity of variance assumption. When the value for *F* is large and the *P*-value is less than .05, the variances are heterogeneous, which violates a key assumption of the *t*-test. The next section of the output provides the actual *t*-test results in two formats. The first row for "Equal" variances is the standard *t*-test taught in introductory statistics. This is the test result that should be reported in a research report under most circumstances. The second row reports a *t*-test for "Equal variances not assumed." This reports an alternative way of computing the *t*-test that accounts for heterogeneous variances and provides an accurate result when the homogeneity assumption has been violated (as indicated by the Levene test). It is rare that one needs to consider using the "Unequal" variances results because, even when the homogeneity assumption is violated, the results are practically indistinguishable. When the "Equal" variances and "Unequal" variances formats lead to different conclusions, seek consultation. The output for both formats shows the degrees of freedom (*df*) and probability (2-tailed significance). As in all statistical tests, the basic criterion for statistical significance is a "2-tailed significance" less than .05. The .865 probability in this example is clearly greater than .05 so the difference is *NOT* statistically significant. The "Mean Difference" statistic indicates the average difference between means. When combined with the confidence interval for the difference, this information can be used to illustrate the variability of the findings.

A second method of performing an independent groups *t*-test with SPSS is to use a quantitative or ordinal variable to divide the dependent or test variable (college GPA in this example) into groups. For example, the group of participants could be divided into two groups by placing those with a high number of study hours per week in one group and a low number of study hours in the second group. Note that this approach would begin with the same information that could be used in computing a correlation. Converting the Studyhrs data to a categorical variable causes some information to be lost. For this reason, caution (and consultation) is needed before using this method. To request the analysis, click **Statistics → Compare Means → Independent Samples T Test...**. Colgpa will remain the "Test Variable(s)" so it can be left where it is. Click "BioSex(1,2)" to highlight it and remove it from the "Grouping Variable" box by clicking the bottom arrow which now faces left because a variable in the input box has been highlighted. Next, highlight "Studyhrs" and move it into the "Grouping Variable" box. Now click **Define Groups...** and click the **Cut point** button. Enter a value (20 in this case) into the box. All participants with values less than the cut point will be in one group and participants with values greater than or equal to the Cut point will form the other group. Click **Continue → OK** and the output will quickly appear. Use the information in the **Group Statistics** table to confirm that the Cut point was selected correctly.

After the analysis is performed it is necessary to compute the effect size for the difference between the two means. Unfortunately, SPSS does not provide this information. However, it can be calculated from the information provided in the SPSS output. A more convenient way to calculate a standardized effect size is to use this Internet site: http://www.cedu.niu.edu/~walker/calculators/effect.asp. This site computes Cohen's *d* using the means, standard deviations, and sample sizes for the two groups as input. I recommend reporting the output for Hedges' *g*, which would be consistent with current practice.

Describing Your Results
After the analysis is complete, results will usually be reported in a paper or publication. The example below describes the results of a *t*-test that resulted in a statistically significant difference. The actual data were from a small survey that was conducted to create a real example for a statistics class. The number in parentheses immediately after the *t* value is degrees of freedom. Power for the study was estimated using tables that appear in Aron et al. (2011).

> Alpha was set at .05. The difference between self-reported total weekly study hours for men ($M = 11.91$; $SD = 7.32$) and women ($M = 20.00$; $SD = 8.29$) was statistically significant, $t(43) = 3.31$, $p = .002$. The effect size was 1.02, which is very large. Given the effect size, power for this study was likely to have been well above .80.

If a study has many *t*-test results to report for different dependent variables and the same independent variable, the findings are often presented in a table. Each row would summarize the results of the *t*-test for one dependent variable. The columns would then show the details of the results. Typically, this would include the mean of each group (with the standard deviation in parentheses), the obtained value for *t*, the sample size, the probability with NS indicating results that were not statistically significant, and the effect size, that is, Cohen's *d* or Hedges' *g*. Note that the distinction between Cohen's *d* or Hedges' *g* is ignored by most writers. The sample size can be indicated in a note to the table if all are the same. If a researcher is planning to publish a study for which a table of *t*-test results will be presented, it may be helpful to look at the journal to which a submission is planned for examples. Some publications may require the confidence interval for the mean difference.

How Does the *t*-test for Independent Groups Work?
The independent groups *t*-test is the heart of many statistics courses, because it can be used for testing associations (i.e., between two measured variables) and for testing causal claims when the independent variable is randomly assigned. Like all parametric tests, the *t*-test for independent groups uses sample data to make inferences about the population using NHST logic. If there is a low probability ($p < .05$) of obtaining the *t*-value, the null hypothesis is rejected, and the research hypothesis is supported. To assess the probability of the obtained *t*-value, the characteristics of the underlying distribution need to be estimated. The underlying distribution is called a distribution of differences between

means. If you wanted to create such a distribution, you would program a computer to take pairs of random samples from a defined population with a known mean and standard deviation. Then the difference between the two means would be computed and plotted in a frequency distribution. If the samples come from the same population (or different populations with the same mean and standard deviation), the average difference between the means will be zero. By assuming zero difference between the populations (i.e., the null hypothesis), we know the mean of the distribution is zero. In order to fully specify the distribution and compute the probability of obtaining a particular value, one only needs to estimate the standard deviation of the underlying distribution of differences between means.

Many statistics students learn how to calculate this standard deviation, and many learn how to turn over the calculations to a computer program such as SPSS. The calculations are somewhat tedious but not extremely difficult. They begin with calculating the variance for each of the two samples. Then these variances are added together or pooled in a way that gives more weight to the sample with the largest sample size. Weighting is accomplished by multiplying each variance by a fraction which is the degrees of freedom for the sample ($N - 1$) divided by the total degrees of freedom ($N_1 - 1 + N_2 - 1$). The formula for the pooled variance estimate looks like this:

$$S^2_{Pooled} = df_1/df_{total}(S^2_1) + df_2/df_{total}(S^2_2)$$

Then we obtain the variances for the distribution of means for each sample. We obtain the variance for the distribution of means of the first sample by dividing S^2_{pooled} by N_1 to obtain S^2_{M1}. Then we obtain the variance for the distribution of means of the second sample by dividing S^2_{pooled} by N_2 to obtain S^2_{M2}. Next, we add S^2_{M1} and S^2_{M2}, and take the square root and we have S_{diff}, which is the standard deviation of the distribution of differences between means. Now we have the mean and standard deviation of the underlying distribution. The shape is a t-distribution with degrees of freedom equal to df_{total}. In order to find the value of t, the difference between the two sample means is divided by S_{diff}. Practically speaking, it would be extremely rare for anyone other than a student taking an exam in a statistics course to compute a t-test by hand. Yet, a little bit of knowledge about the computations helps in understanding two key issues.

Effect Size and Confidence Intervals for the Independent Groups t-test
When using SPSS, the effect size for an independent groups t-test must be calculated manually or with an online calculator such as this one, developed by David Walker. Although I have been calling the effect size measure for the independent groups t-test, Cohen's d, as do most other authors, technically it should be known as Hedges' g. The difference between the two is that Cohen's d uses the sample size (not N -1) in computing the sample variances, whereas Hedges' g uses $N - 1$. Today's custom is to refer to the effect size measure for the difference between means as Cohen's d (Grissom & Kim, 2012), even though the actual calculations follow the correction employed in Hedges' g. Thus, if one were calculating Cohen's d by hand, they would use the descriptive statistics output for SPSS, square the standard deviations to obtain variances, enter the variances into the formula for S^2_{pooled} and then take the square root to obtain the standard deviation of the individual difference scores, S_{pooled}. The effect size is the difference between the sample means ($M_1 - M_2$) divided by S_{pooled}.

The meaning of d is that it represents degree of difference between groups in standard deviation units relative to the distribution of *individual* scores. By convention, small, medium, and large effect sizes for d are .20, .50, and .80, respectively. Figure 8-2 shows two hypothetical population distributions with a d of .50. The illustration is not very impressive because there is about a 67% overlap between the two distributions.

Figure 8-2. Illustration of Medium Effect Size, *d*

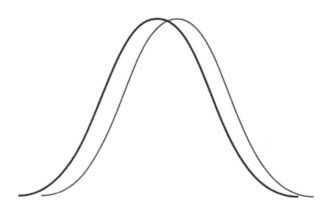

Another way to think about effect size is in terms of individual change. Imagine that a study of teaching reading included an experimental group and a control group and that the study produced an effect size of .55 in favor of the experimental group. Looking at Figure 8-1, one might not be very impressed by such results. On the other hand, on average an individual child would improve by .55 standard deviations. For a child starting the study at the 50th percentile, the treatment would be associated with an improvement to the 71st percentile, but more important, a child starting at the 29th percentile could improve to an average score. While the group difference does not look impressive, individual change can have an important impact.

Like other statistical results, effect sizes have variability associated with them, which can be captured by computing a confidence interval. Although confidence intervals and effect sizes for means have become the norm, the demand to provide a confidence interval for effect sizes seems to be lacking at this time. Still, all researchers need to be aware of the variability associated with their data. Even an exact replication of a study is highly unlikely to produce identical results, therefore it makes sense to briefly discuss the confidence interval for an effect size. Howell (n.d.) provides an excellent discussion of this topic. The confidence interval around the effect size is not symmetrical, unlike the confidence interval around the difference between means (see next section). It involves what is called, the noncentral *t*-distribution. A central *t*-distribution has a symmetrical distribution around zero, whereas a noncentral *t*-distribution is asymmetrical because it is not distributed around zero. Howell describes how to compute the confidence interval around a noncentral *t*-distribution, but he also refers readers to programs that are available online for performing the computations. One such program is available here. Using this program written by James Uanhoro, I calculated the 95% CI for the effect size of .0722 and found it to be [.93088, -.7825]. Had this example been a real research study these results would be very discouraging; not only is the confidence interval very wide, it includes the possibility of a zero effect size. However, this is what happens when a study is run with a very small number of subjects, and a very small effect size (.0722) is obtained.

What about the difference between means? Does this difference also have a confidence interval? Unlike, confidence intervals for *r*, the correlation coefficient, and *d*, the effect size, the confidence interval for the difference is easily accessible in the SPSS output. As noted above in the discussion of how the *t*-test for independent means works, the comparison distribution is a distribution of differences between means with a mean of zero, under the null hypothesis. The test statistic is computed by dividing the difference between the sample means by S_{diff} which is the standard deviation of the distribution of differences between means. William S. Gosset developed the *t*-distribution which could be used with small sample studies, unlike the normal or *z*-distribution. The test is often called Student's *t*-test, after the pseudonym that Gosset used to disguise his association with the Guinness Brewery. The independent groups *t*-test uses the *t*-distribution to determine whether the sample difference is rare enough (p < .05) that it supports rejection of the null hypothesis of no difference, thereby supporting the research hypothesis that the obtained sample difference is not the result of chance or random variation. SPSS output provides the probability of obtaining the difference through chance or random variation under "Sig. (2-tailed)" and the confidence interval under "95% Confidence Interval of the Difference." Both the probability and the confidence interval for the difference are based upon the same information and lead to the same conclusion. The 95% CI [-.71758, .60849] shows that the population value for the difference between means has a 95% chance of being found between -.71758 and .60849. Consistent with the fact that this result is not statistically significant ($p = .865$), the confidence interval for the difference between means is very wide and includes zero. For studies that are statistically significant, the confidence interval will not contain zero. As discussed previously, some authors (e.g., Cuming, 2014) believe that reporting probabilities and NHST should be abandoned in favor of presenting confidence intervals. However, NHST and summarizing outcomes with the probability of the finding continues to have a strong presence in the research literature with little sign of being replaced.

The *t*-test For Dependent Groups using SPSS

The *t*-test for **dependent** groups requires a different way of approaching the data. For this type of test, each case has two measures of the same variable taken at different times. This is a repeated measures design. In the repeated measures situation, one might collect GPA information at two different points in the careers of a group of students. The table below shows this for a fictional example. In this case, GPA data have been collected at the end of each participant's first year (ColGPA1) and senior year (ColGPA2). The data shown below represent about half of the dataset that was included in the example SPSS computations.

Participant	ColGPA1	Study Hours	Sex	ColGPA2
Participant #01	1.8	15	2	.
Participant #02	3.9	38	1	3.9
Participant #03	2.1	10	2	2.8
Participant #04	2.8	24	1	3.2
Participant #05	3.3	36	.	3.6
Participant #06	3.1	15	2	3.6
Participant #07	4.0	45	1	4.0
Participant #08	3.4	28	1	3.4
Participant #09	3.3	35	1	3.7
Participant #10	2.2	10	2	2.6
Participant #11	2.5	6	2	2.7

Note that ColGPA2 of the first participant is missing. Given the 1.8 GPA at the first assessment, it seems reasonable that this person might not remain in college for the entire four years. This is a common hazard of repeated measures designs, and the implication of missing data needs to be considered before interpreting the results. For example, if a researcher conducts a study of the efficacy of treatment for depression, it could be the case that those who drop out of treatment became discouraged when the treatment did not work for them. This would require thoughtful interpretation of the data for those who remain in the study.

To request the analysis, click **_Analyze_** → **_Compare Means_** → **_Paired-Samples T Test_** ... A window will appear with a list of variables on the left and a box labeled "Paired Variables" on the right. An example of the input window is shown in Figure 8-3.

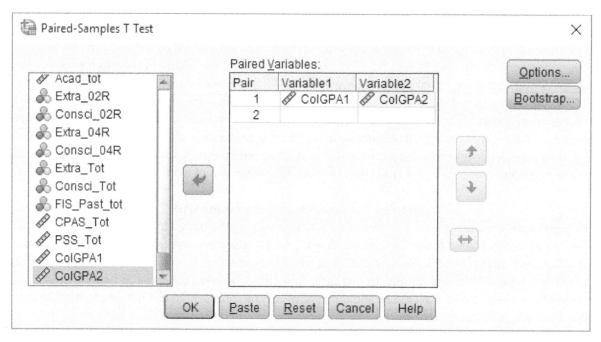

Figure 8-3. Input window for paired-samples or dependent samples _t_-test.

Highlight the first variable of the pair and transfer it to the **_Variable 1_** column of the first row and then transfer the second member of the pair to the **_Variable 2_** column of the first row. Thus, for this example ColGPA1 and ColGPA2 are transferred to the "Paired Variables" box by clicking the right-pointing arrow between the boxes. Several pairs of variables can be entered. The **_Options..._** button opens a window that allows control of the confidence interval and missing data options. Click **Continue** (if you opened the **_Options..._** window) → **_OK_** to complete the analysis. The output will appear in an Output window. Results for the example problem are shown in Tables 8-4a, 8-4b, and 8-4c.

Note that another way to produce paired samples is to begin with two groups of different people and forms pairs of individuals by matching them on a variable the researcher would like to control or hold constant. This procedure is rarely encountered in the modern research literature and will not be discussed further. See Hayes (1988; pp. 313-315) for a more detailed explanation. However, this technique would create pairs of data for each subject as in the current example and analysis would proceed in the same way.

Table 8-4b shows the correlation between ColGPA1 and ColGPA2. The information is not important for interpreting the outcome. However, it indicates the magnitude of the dependence of the two conditions. It is useful information for the statistician who wishes to understand the theory that underlies the computations for the dependent groups _t_-test.

Table 8-4a. Paired Samples Statistics

		Mean	N	Std. Deviation	Std. Error Mean
Pair 1	ColGPA1	2.8800	20	.68411	.15297
	ColGPA2	3.0600	20	.61934	.13849

Table 8-4b. Paired Samples Correlations

		N	Correlation	Sig.
Pair 1	ColGPA1 & ColGPA2	20	.782	.000

Table 8-4c. Paired Samples Test

		Paired Differences							
					95% Confidence Interval of the Difference				
		Mean	Std. Deviation	Std. Error Mean	Lower	Upper	t	df	Sig. (2-tailed)
Pair 1	ColGPA1 - ColGPA2	-.18000	.43480	.09722	-.38349	.02349	-1.851	19	.080

The remaining output is like the independent groups t-test. The first table (8-4a) of output shows the means and standard deviations for the two conditions. Table (8-4c) shows the mean of the differences, standard deviation of the differences, standard error of the mean, the confidence interval for the difference, and the obtained value for t. The 2-tailed Sig[nificance] which is stated as a probability is shown in the last column. As usual, probabilities *less than* .05 indicate that the null hypothesis should be rejected. In this case, the interpretation would be that GPA did not change significantly from first-year to senior year, $t(19) = -1.85$, $p = .080$. It would also be very desirable to compute the effect size (Cohen's d) for this analysis. This can be accomplished using the information in Table 8-4c. The effect size is equal to the mean of paired differences divided by the standard deviation of paired differences. Thus, for Pair 1, d would be equal to -.18000/.43480 = -.4139. This would be between a small and medium effect size (see Table 6-1). Absence of statistical significance and the presence of a nearly medium effect size indicate that the study was under-powered. That is, the researcher should "get more subjects." Inspection of the confidence interval for the difference leads to the same conclusion as the p-value. The 95% CI includes zero, so the result is not statistically significant.

Describing Your Results
To present the results of a dependent groups t-test in a paper, the means and standard deviations of the two conditions (Table 8-3a), the obtained t value, df, and the probability would be reported using a format like the independent groups t-test, as shown in the following example. Note that the sign of the t-test value is omitted because the direction of the difference can be inferred from the means.

> Alpha was set at .05. The difference between college GPA for first-year students ($M = 2.88$; $SD = .684$) and the same students as seniors ($M = 3.06$; $SD = .619$) was not statistically significant, $t(19) = 1.85$, $p = .080$. The effect size was .414, which could be characterized as between a small and medium effect size. Power for this study was approximately .40. About 60 subjects would be needed to reach an adequate level of .80 power.

Analysis of Variance with SPSS
Analysis of variance (ANOVA) is a flexible statistical procedure used when a researcher compares differences among *more than* two means of a quantitative dependent variable. The procedure is incredibly versatile. Two different ANOVA models will be described in *QRST*: the simple one-way ANOVA and the two-way factorial ANOVA. The one-way ANOVA is analogous to the t-test except that *more than two* means can be tested for differences at the same time. For example, to investigate a variable in college students, a researcher may wish to compare averages for first-year, sophomore, junior, and senior students. Because more than two means are being tested, a one-way analysis of variance would be the appropriate test. The final result of an ANOVA is an F-ratio which can be interpreted in the same way as the t-ratio.

However, a significant F-ratio indicates that some difference exists among the tested means. To determine what mean, means, or combination of means differ, it is necessary to employ subsequent tests which can either be planned ahead of time (*a priori*) or after the results have been seen (*post hoc*). The main issue in selecting exactly which test to use is to prevent Type I errors that would result if several tests were conducted without adjusting the alpha level. SPSS has several subsequent test options. Most often, one of the *post hoc* tests is employed such as the Ryan-Einot-Gabriel-Welsch Range test (R-E-G-W-Q).

One-Way ANOVA with SPSS

A one-way (or single-factor) ANOVA begins with data entry. In this example, the dependent variable was a quantitative construct called "Systemic Thinking" (Wielkiewicz, 2000) which reflects the extent to which the individual sees leadership as a complex, multivariate process that works best when all individuals in an organization are given an opportunity to participate. Lower scores indicate a stronger belief that leadership is best approached in a systemic way. The independent variable was academic class. Data entry would proceed as with the *t*-test. The dependent variable would be in one column and the grouping variable in another column. The difference is that the grouping variable has four possible codes. In the example, the independent or grouping variable was whether the individual reported being a first-year, sophomore, junior, or senior student. The analysis begins by entering the data into the SPSS spreadsheet as described previously. Two variables are required: a dependent variable and a grouping variable. The variables can then be named and labeled as appropriate. To conduct a one-way ANOVA, click *Analyze* → *Compare Means* → *One-Way ANOVA...*. This will open a simple input box. Transfer the dependent variable(s) into the *Dependent List* box and the grouping or independent variable to the *Factor* box. If the factor includes a code that is not needed because too few participants were in one of the categories or a category had a label such as "Does Not Apply" or "Don't Know" in which the researcher was not interested, a recode (described below) of the variable may be needed. Then click the *Post Hoc...* button and select the tests that look interesting and then *Continue*. Then click the *Options...* button and select *Descriptives* and the *Homogeneity of variance test* then *Continue*. At this point, you are ready to click *OK* and execute the analysis. Confidence intervals are available from the normal output of this analysis so the bootstrapping feature is not necessary.

Descriptive statistics for the one-way ANOVA are shown in Table 8-5a. The first three columns (*N*, Mean, & Std. Deviation) are self-explanatory. The Std. Error is the standard error of the mean, that is the standard deviation for the distribution of means and is used to construct the confidence interval around the mean, shown in the next two columns. Thus, the 95% confidence interval for the sample mean of 26.1301 (First-year college students) is 25.1176 to 27.1427. The confidence interval for these means is interpreted somewhat differently compared to the output of the *t*-test. The confidence intervals of the ANOVA means are compared to each other instead of zero. For example, the 95% CI [25.12, 27.14] for first-year students has no overlap with the Senior students (95% CI [22.43, 24.72]). Therefore, it is reasonable to conclude that these means (26.13 and 23.56) come from different populations. It can be tedious to compare each confidence interval, with the others. An alternative approach is to use SPSS to construct a visual representation of the information, which is described below.

Table 8-5a. Descriptives for One-Way ANOVA
LabsSysThinkTot

	N	Mean	Std. Deviation	Std. Error	95% Confidence Interval for Mean Lower Bound	Upper Bound	Min	Max
First-year	146	26.1301	6.19039	.51232	25.1176	27.1427	14.00	66.00
Sophomore	130	27.2231	5.48467	.48104	26.2713	28.1748	14.00	51.00
Junior	93	24.9677	5.02050	.52060	23.9338	26.0017	14.00	36.00
Senior	69	23.5797	4.76632	.57380	22.4347	24.7247	14.00	34.00
Total	438	25.8059	5.65696	.27030	25.2747	26.3372	14.00	66.00

The SPSS results of the ANOVA are shown in Table 8-5b.

Table 8-5b. ANOVA Results

LabsSysThinkTot

	Sum of Squares	Df	Mean Square	F	Sig.
Between Groups	683.732	3	227.911	7.437	.000
Within Groups	13300.773	434	30.647		
Total	13984.505	437			

The ANOVA table is easy to understand. The most important part of the table is the first row, which shows the effect of the independent variable. "Sum of Squares" is the numerator from the variance computations and could be used to compute the F-ratio by hand. The df column is important because the first two values are needed to report the ANOVA results in an article or report for a class. The "mean square" column shows the variances that are used to compute the F-ratio. You can check this by dividing the two numbers yourself. The F column shows the value of the F-ratio and should be reported in any empirical papers you write about the results. The Sig. column shows the probability associated with this F-ratio. If the value is less than .05, the NH is rejected. These results are obviously statistically significant.

The output for the R-E-G-W-Q test is shown in Table 8-5c.

Table 8-5c. LabsSysThinkTot

Ryan-Einot-Gabriel-Welsch Range[a]

		Subset for alpha = 0.05		
CollYr_Recode	N	1	2	3
Senior	69	23.5797		
Junior	93	24.9677	24.9677	
First-year	146		26.1301	26.1301
Sophomore	130			27.2231
Sig.		.263	.282	.212

Means for groups in homogeneous subsets are displayed.

Critical values are not monotonic for these data. Substitutions have been made to ensure monotonicity. Type I error is therefore smaller.

The columns labeled 1, 2, and 3 show which means group into homogeneous subsets. In other words, each subset consists of means that are not significantly different from *each other* but are significantly different from the *other subsets*. The first subset consists of Seniors and Juniors which have means that are close to each other but different from the other two subsets. The way the results are presented is a nice summary of what one needs to know about the individual group means, which ones are the same and which ones are different from each other.

Previously, interpretation of the confidence intervals for the means was discussed. Although the confidence intervals in Table 8-5a can be compared, a visual representation may be more appealing. Although it is possible to request a plot of the means using the SPSS routine for One-way ANOVA, there is another way to request the same plot. To obtain this output, click **Graphs → Legacy Dialogs → Bar...** and click the box labeled **Simple.** Once this box is highlighted, click

Define and a new dialog box will appear. Figure 8-4 shows the dialogue box for a simple bar graph of the means in the presence example. Begin by choosing the "bar represents mean" option. Then move variables into the appropriate boxes. Move the dependent variable, Systemic Thinking (LabsSysThinkTot) into the *Line Represents ... Variable*: box by highlighting the variable name and clicking the right-facing arrow. Then select the *Category Axis* variable (in this case, ColYr_Recode) and move it into the box. Then click the *Options* button on the right, which opens another dialog box. In this dialogue box, click the box labeled *Display error bars* and leave the default option of 95% confidence intervals untouched. Click *Continue* and *OK*, and the results will be displayed almost instantly. They are shown below in Figure 8-5. With the 95% confidence intervals displayed graphically, it is possible to see the differences among the means more clearly. For comparison, Figure 8-6 shows a plot of the means obtained via the *One-way ANOVA....* subroutine. If the error bars overlap, it is an indication that the means come from the same population, and are not difference from each other.

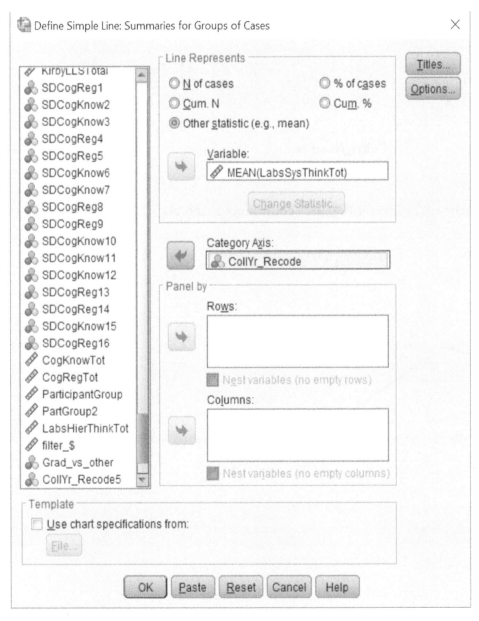

Figure 8-4. Dialog box for creating a bar graph.

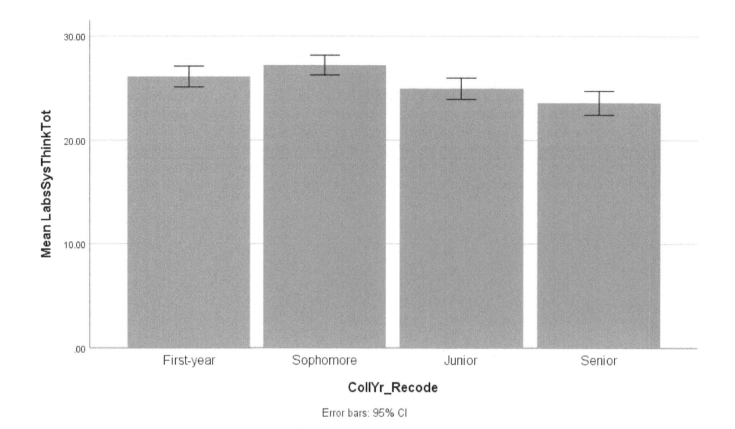

Figure 8-5. Bar graph of means with error bars representing 95% confidence intervals.

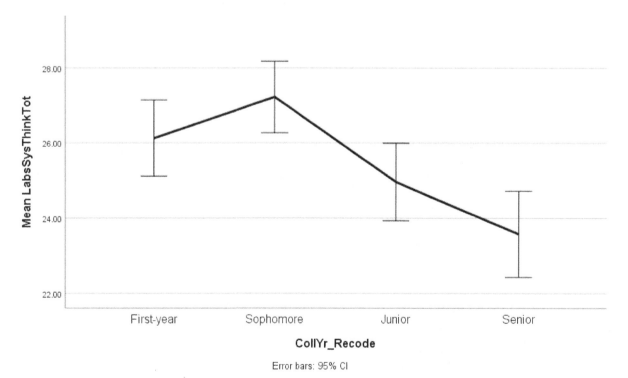

Figure 8-6. Line graph with 95% confidence intervals.

Reporting Your Results

One way to report these results in an article would be like this:

> The means for First-years ($M = 26.13$; $SD = 6.19$), Sophomores ($M = 27.22$; $SD = 5.48$), Juniors ($M = 24.96$; $SD = 5.02$), and Seniors ($M = 23.56$; $SD = 4.77$) were significantly different $F(3, 434) = 7.44$, $p = .000$. A Ryan-Einot-Gabriel-Welsch Range test showed that the means grouped into three homogeneous subsets: Seniors and Juniors, Juniors and First-years, and First-years and Sophomores. Thus, older students tended to have a more systemic view of leadership.

There is an interesting note about the probability for this analysis. Some reviewers argue that $p = .000$ is not a valid expression because it implies the probability is exactly equal to zero. They argue that the probability should be $p < .001$. My own view is that $p = .000$ is valid because it approximates the exact value. Because the result is presented to three decimal places, the fourth decimal place and beyond are left ambiguous. Thus, $p = .000$ does not mean the probability is exactly zero.

Factorial ANOVA with SPSS

Factorial analysis of variance is an extension of the one-way analysis. The difference is that a factorial analysis has more than one *independent* (grouping) variable. The example is a 2 X 2 analysis of variance. This can also be called a factorial analysis of variance, which is a generic term that applies to many designs. The two independent variables are Gender (male vs. female) and the students' answers to a question asking whether they sent text messages while in class. The dependent variable was the student's self-reported cumulative college GPA. Factorial ANOVA procedures can become very complex due to the assumptions involved and the variety of methods available for computing the analysis. Generally, researchers should try to have the same number of participants in each cell of the design, if possible. When the cells have unequal numbers of participants, the danger of assumptions being violated is greater, and the available options for computing the analysis are the most variable. However, even when the cells contain unequal numbers of participants, the default options (those automatically available from SPSS) provide good solutions.

To conduct this analysis, three pieces of information about each participant are needed, their GPA, gender, and in-class texting habits. To prepare these data for analysis, the information about each participant (GPA, gender, texting) needs to be arranged horizontally with one row of data for each participant as in previous examples. The data below illustrate what the input would look like for the first eight subjects. Adding variable names and variable labels makes the output easier to interpret. These tasks can be accomplished using the procedures described earlier. The next task is to request that the analysis of variance be performed.

Participant #	GPA	Gender	Texting in Class
#1	3.2	1	1
#2	3.1	2	1
#3	3.3	1	2
#4	3.4	2	2
#5	3.2	1	1
#6	3.3	2	1
#7	3.3	1	2
#8	3.2	2	2

To do the analysis, select **_Analyze_** → **_General Linear Model_** → **_Univariate_**... An input window will appear. Highlight the dependent variable (GPA, in this case) and transfer it to the **_Dependent_** box and highlight the independent or grouping variables and transfer them to the "Fixed Factor(s)" box. At this point the **OK** button will be available. Clicking it will produce the desired analysis using the default settings that the SPSS program provides. Figure 8-7 shows the input window for this analysis.

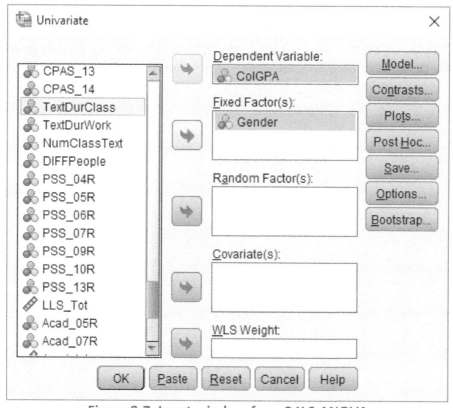

Figure 8-7. Input window for a 2 X 2 ANOVA

Then, some interesting choices need to be made. Clicking the **Options...** button reveals several useful outputs such as means, frequency counts, observed power, and effect sizes. Create a plot of the interaction means by placing Gender variable in the **Separate Lines** box, and the T/F question about texting in the **Horizontal Axis** box. You may need to reverse these entries if you are not happy with the appearance of the output when you analyze your own data. Click **Add** and **Continue** to get to the main input box and **OK** to view the output. The plot will show "Estimated Marginal Means" instead of the exact means from the descriptive statistics. The estimated means and descriptive statistics would be the same if the cells of the design contained equal numbers of subjects. Tables 8-6a and 8-6b show the results for the example, based upon a large sample of participants. Figure 8-9 shows the plot of the means produced by SPSS.

Figure 8-9 illustrates the problems associated with unequal sample sizes in a factorial design. To understand what is going on, it is necessary to review calculation of the mean. This is the key to comprehending the various statistical approaches to computing an analysis of variance. Imagine a sample that consists of the heights (in inches) of six males: 73, 76, 69, 71, 68, and 75 inches. The mean is the sum of the scores divided by the sample size:

$$M = \frac{\sum X}{N} = 432/6 = 72.0$$

Imagine a second sample that consists of heights of two females: 62 and 64 inches. The mean is the sum of the scores divided by the sample size:

$$M = \frac{\sum X}{N} = 126/2 = 63.0$$

Now, imagine that the researcher desires to know the overall mean of the 6 males and 2 females. There are two equally valid ways to compute this "grand" mean. One way is to add up all scores and divide by eight:

$$M = \frac{\sum X}{N} = (73 + 76 + 69 + 71 + 68 + 75 + 62 + 64) /8 = 69.75$$

This is the *weighted means* average because the group with the largest number of subjects (males) gets more weight because of having more subjects. There is another way to compute the mean of all subjects called the *unweighted* average. This is the average of the two group means:

$$M = \frac{\sum X}{N} = (72.0 + 63.0)/2 = 67.5$$

Note that the weighted and unweighted averages result in different values for the combined or "grand" mean. If the same number of individuals were in each group, both methods would yield the same result. When one group has more subjects, that group receives more "weight" in the computations when all the individual heights are added and divided by eight. The best approach to conducting an ANOVA is to have equal numbers of subjects in all the cells. When there are equal sample sizes in each cell of the design, these complications disappear; the weighted and unweighted computations of the means produce the same results. However, *unequal* sample sizes create some interesting issues in computing and interpreting a factorial ANOVA. Unequal sample sizes create two valid methods of computing the ANOVA and it disrupts the independence of the two factors. In other words, the factors or independent variables are not **orthogonal**. Instead, they correlate with each other, making it difficult to divide the variances in the analysis and assign them to the appropriate main effect or interaction. Tabachnick and Fidell (2007, 2013) put this computation question very succinctly (p. 219) when they state, "Is the marginal mean the mean of the means, or is it the mean of the scores?"

This creates practical issues in the computation and interpretation of factorial ANOVA. First, there are two ways to compute the means, the weighted and unweighted approaches. Thus, it is not surprising that requests for the ANOVA means can show different results, depending upon what was requested. Table 8-6a shows the descriptive statistics for the example ANOVA. Note that the means are different than those shown in Figure 8-9, which shows "estimated marginal means." For example, the mean in Table 8-5a for males who text is 2.925, whereas the same mean in Figure 8-3c is about 3.13. The reasons these means are different is that the means in Table 8-6a are descriptive statistics calculated using the weighted method, whereas the means in Figure 8-9 are calculated using the unweighted approach. Which of these two approaches is best?

The default option is to use the unweighted approach, called a Type III sum of squares. This is seen Table 8-6b, which shows the ANOVA result for the example. Note that Column 3 is labeled "Type III Sum of Squares" indicating that the calculations were based on the unweighted approach. This is the default (automatic) method in SPSS and is the most common approach to computing an ANOVA. According to Tabachnick and Fidell (2013), the Type III Sum of Squares is a conservative method that is unlikely to be criticized. However, treating all cells as though sample sizes were equal (the unweighted approach) may not make sense when unequal sample sizes actually reflect the populations from which the samples were drawn. For example, females may be more prevalent in both the sample and the population. In such a case, the weighted means approach might be justified. This is accomplished by requesting a Type I Sum of Squares. The way to do this is go to **_Analyze_** → **_General Linear Model_** → **_Univariate_**.... Then click the **_Model_** button on the right. This will open the widow shown in Figure 8-8. On the lower left is the drop-down menu that allows the researcher to change the method of calculation from Type III (default) to Type I. Note that it is also possible to remove the intercept from the model using this window. Figure 8-9 shows the plot of the estimated marginal means created by SPSS.

One effective option for dealing with these choices is to select "all of the above." That is, conduct the ANOVA using the default Type III Sum of Squares option. Then, run the analysis again using the Type I Sum of Squares. Chances are that both analyses will support the same conclusions, especially given medium to large sample sizes. If the two methods result in different conclusions, do additional research and thinking to determine which of the methods should be reported, keeping in mind that the Type III Sum of Squares will rarely face criticism. I did exactly this for the example analysis and it made minor differences in the numerical values but no difference in interpretation. The two main effects were statistically significant but not the interaction using both the Type III and Type I Sum of Squares computations.

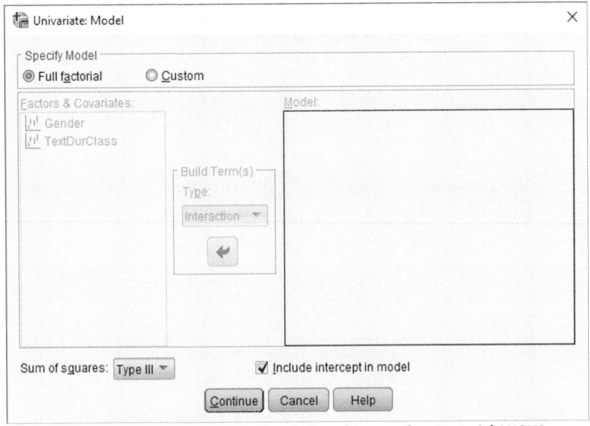

Figure 8-8. Specifying Type III or Type I Sum of Squares for a Factorial ANOVA

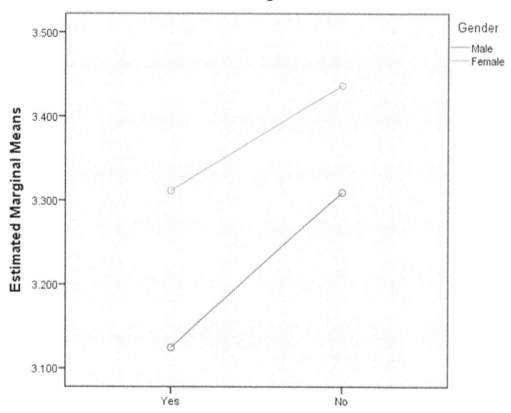

Figure 8-9. Plot of interaction means created by SPSS

Table 8-6a. Descriptive Statistics
Dependent Variable: Please enter your cumulative GPA in the box

Gender	Do you send text messages regularly during classes?	Mean	Std. Deviation	N
Male	Yes	2.9250	.58051	22
	No	3.2980	.44009	166
	Total	3.2543	.47243	188
Female	Yes	3.1643	.43873	40
	No	3.4168	.41290	239
	Total	3.3806	.42523	279
Total	Yes	3.0794	.50239	62
	No	3.3681	.42774	405
	Total	3.3298	.44864	467

Table 8-6a shows the descriptive statistics calculated using the weighted means method. It might appear to be a little challenging to read, but careful examination shows that each condition is clearly labeled. For example, the first mean (M = 2.9250) is the mean of males who answered "Yes" to the question about sending text messages while in class. The next mean (M = 3.2980) is the mean of males who answered "No" to the texting question. [Note the large difference here! The ES is .81, large by Cohen's standards.] The third mean (M = 3.2543) is the mean for all males regardless of how they answered the texting question. The next three means (3.1643, 3.4168, & 3.3806) show the same means for females. The box labeled "Total" has three means. The first mean (M = 3.0794) is the mean of all people who answered "YES" to the texting question regardless of their gender. The next mean (M = 3.3681) is the mean of all people who answered "NO" to the texting question regardless of their gender. The last mean (Total Total; M = 3.3298) is the mean of all subjects regardless of condition and is referred to as the Grand Mean in textbooks. It is also possible to request the "Estimated" marginal means in SPSS.

Table 8-6b shows the output for this analysis. A Type III Sum of Squares, the default option, was computed. Note that I shortened the names of the variables to make the table easier to read. I also numbered the columns (C) and rows (R) so I could refer to them in the text.

Table 8-6b. Tests of Between-Subjects Effects
Dependent Variable: Please enter your cumulative GPA in the box

Source (C1)	Type III Sum of Squares (C2)	Df (C3)	Mean Square (C4)	F (C4)	Sig. (C5)	Partial Eta Squared (C6)
Corrected Model (R1)	6.679[a]	3	2.226	11.833	.000	.071
Intercept (R2)	2032.450	1	2032.450	10801.793	.000	.959
Gender (R3)	1.590	1	1.590	8.450	.004	.018
TextRegularlyInClasses (R4)	4.851	1	4.851	25.780	.000	.053
Gender * TextInClasses (R5)	.180	1	.180	.955	.329	.002
Error (R6)	87.117	463	.188			
Total (R7)	5271.581	467				
Corrected Total (R8)	93.797	466				

a. R Squared = .071 (Adjusted R Squared = .065)

Something I learned as a graduate student was this: "Statistical programs are easy to use if you ignore what you don't need to know." This advice applies to interpreting this SPSS output; if you ignore what you don't need to know, it is much easier to understand. Thus, it is a good idea to ignore R1, R2, R7, R8, C2, and C4 because they provide information that you don't need to know, unless you are a mathematical statistician or specialist. So, what *do* you need to know from this table? C5 shows probabilities for the effects evaluated in the model. Rows 3, 4, and 5 provide information about the main effects and the interaction. So, looking at the intersection of rows 3, 4, and 5 with column 5, the researcher can determine what effects are statistically significant. In this analysis, both main effects (Gender and Text Regularly, R4 and R5) are statistically significant. The interaction (Gender * TextRegularly, R5) is NOT statistically significant. C6 ("Partial Eta Squared") is an effect size measure that is interpreted like a squared correlation coefficient. Small, medium, and large effect sizes for partial eta squared are .01, .06, and .14, respectively. Thus, the main effect of texting has close to a medium effect size. C3 shows degrees of freedom, which are reported for each effect. As noted previously, I also ran this analysis using computations for Type I Sum of Squares and obtained similar results.

Reporting Your Results
To report a factorial ANOVA in a research article, report each significant effect providing the same information as for a one-way ANOVA. If you stick with the default option of using the Type III Sum of Squares, it is not necessary to state this

in the report. The means can be reported in a table or in the text depending upon which reporting method is most efficient. If the interaction is statistically significant, a graphic presentation is typical. Interpreting a statistically significant interaction takes precedence over the main effects. There are many ways to present these results and one example is shown below. Note that Figure 8-10 uses the means from the descriptive statistics (therefore, weighted). This reflects my personal bias to report the actual, obtained data as opposed to reporting data with an "adjustment." This approach is supported by the fact that Figures 8-9 and 8-10 are very similar and lead to the same conclusions.

A 2 (Gender) X 2 (Texting) analysis of variance was conducted with college GPA as the dependent measure. The main effect of Gender was statistically significant, $F(1, 463) = 8.45$, $p = .004$, indicating that the means for males ($M = 3.25$; $SD = .472$) and females ($M = 3.38$; $SD = .425$) were significantly different. Similarly, the main effect means for the texting group ($M = 3.08$; $SD = .502$) and the no texting group ($M = 3.37$; $SD = .428$) differed significantly, $F(1, 463) = 4.85$, $p = .000$. Partial eta squared values for gender and texting were .018 and .053, respectively. The interaction was not statistically significant, $F(1, 463) = .955$, $p = .585$. The interaction is shown in Figure 8-10. [Note: In APA style, figures are numbered consecutively as they appear in the article. Thus, the technically correct way to refer to this figure in an article is Figure 1, assuming it is the first figure to appear in the article. There would be no need to include a figure for a nonsignificant interaction. The plot of the adjusted means created by SPSS can also be used to display results.]

Had the interaction between gender and texting been statistically significant, the most common way to illustrate the nature of the interaction is with a line or bar graph. Because the interaction is not statistically significant in this case, the lines are almost perfectly parallel. A statistically significant interaction would have lines that were NOT parallel. The graph shown in Figure 8-10 was created with a word-processing program using the means from the descriptive statistics.

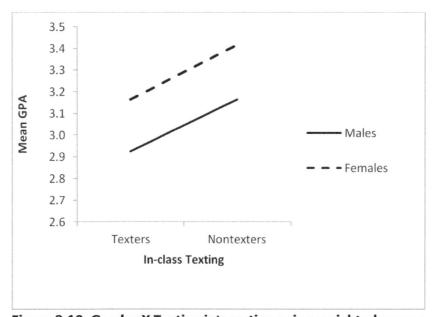

Figure 8-10. Gender X Texting interaction using weighted means.

There are a couple of options for obtaining confidence intervals for a factorial ANOVA. Figure 8-11 shows one such example. This graph was created by clicking **Graphs → Legacy Dialogs → Line … Multiple**. Then click the **Define** button to produce another dialog box shown in Figure 8-12. Click the "Other statistic (e.g., mean)" button and leave the default option untouched. Enter the factors into **Category Axis:** and **Define Lines by:**, adjusting the entries later if the appearance of the graph is not satisfactory. The click the **Options …** button and select **Display error bars** to obtain the output, using the default 95% CI option. Means with confidence intervals for the main effects can be created using bar graphs, as described earlier in the section on the independent groups t-test. Tabachnick and Fidell (2007, pp. 40-43) describe how to compute confidence intervals by hand for each mean, using the distribution of means and the t-

distribution. Note that there were no subsequent tests in this example because the independent variables have two levels.

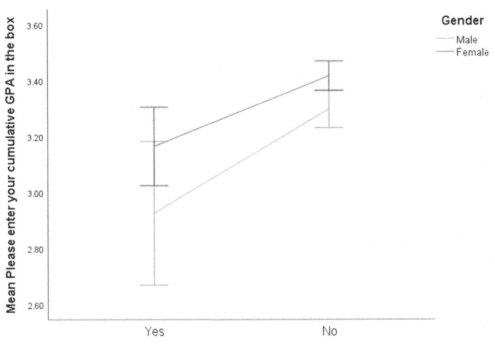

Figure 8-11. Plot of interaction means created with the graphing subroutine of SPSS

Figure 8-12. Dialog box for creating graph of interaction means with 95% CIs.

Chi-Square with SPSS

The chi-square goodness of fit test and test for independence are used for analyzing whether a frequency distribution for a categorical (i.e., nominal) variable is consistent with expectations (a goodness of fit test), or whether two categorical (nominal) variables are related or associated with each other (a test for independence). Categorical variables assign values by virtue of being a member of a category. Sex is a nominal variable. For a majority of individuals, it can take on two values, male and female, which are usually coded numerically as 1 or 2. These numerical codes do not give any information about how much of some characteristic the individual possesses. Instead, the numbers provide information about the category to which the individual belongs. Other examples of nominal or categorical variables include hair color, race, diagnosis (e.g., ADHD vs. anxiety vs. depression vs. chemically dependent), and type of treatment (e.g., medication vs. behavior management vs. none). Note that these are the same types of variables that can be used as independent variables in a t-test or ANOVA. In ANOVA, the researcher is interested in the means of a quantitative variable. In chi-square, the interest is in the frequency with which individuals fall in the category or combination of categories. Another perspective on this difference is that the dependent variable for a chi-square analysis is the frequency count for each cell or category, whereas for an analysis of variance the dependent variable is a quantitative measure for which it makes sense to compute a mean.

Chi-Square Test for Goodness of Fit

A chi-square test for goodness of fit can be requested by clicking **_Analyze_ → _Nonparametric Tests_ → _Legacy Dialogs_ → _Chi-square_**. This opens a window like other tests. Enter the variable to be tested into the **_Test Variable_** box. Then a decision about the expected values against which the actual frequencies are to be tested needs to be made. The most common choice is "All categories equal." However, it is also possible to enter specific expected values by checking the other circle and entering expected values in order. The expected values used in computing the chi-square will be proportional to these values. The **Options...** button provides access to missing value options and descriptive statistics for each variable. To submit the analysis, click the **OK** button. Tables 8-7a and 8-7b show results for a chi-square goodness of fit test.

Table 8-7a. BioSex

	Observed N	Expected N	Residual
Male	11	13.0	-2.0
female	15	13.0	2.0
Total	26		

Table 8-7b. Test Statistics

	BioSex
Chi-Square	.615[a]
Df	1
Asymp. Sig.	.433

a. 0 cells (0.0%) have expected frequencies less than 5. The minimum expected cell frequency is 13.0.

The value under "Chi-Square" is .615. As usual, statistically significant results are indicated by "Asymp. Sig." values below .05. Obviously, this example is *NOT* statistically significant. In words, these results indicate that the obtained frequencies do not differ significantly from those that would be expected if all cell frequencies were equal in the population.

Chi-Square Test for Independence

The chi-square test for independence is a test of whether *two* categorical variables are associated with each other. For example, imagine that a survey of approximately 200 individuals has been conducted and that 120 of these people report being females and 80 report being males. Now, assume that the survey includes information about each individual's major in college. To keep the example simple, assume that each person is either a psychology or a biology major. It might be asked whether males and females tend to choose these two majors at about the same rate or does one of the majors have a different proportion of one sex than the other major. Table 8-8a shows the case where males and females tend to be about equally represented in the two majors. In this case, college major is *independent* of sex. Note that the percentage of females in psychology and biology is 59.8 and 60.2, respectively. Another way to characterize these data is to say that sex and major are independent of each other because the proportion of males and females remains the same for both majors.

Table 8-8a. Hypothetical Frequency Data		
	Psychology Majors	Biology Majors
Females	58	62
Males	39	41

The next example shows the same problem with a different result. In the hypothetical data shown in Table 8-8b, the proportion of males and females *depends* upon the major. Females compose 79.6 percent of psychology majors and only 39.2 percent of biology majors. Clearly, the proportion of each sex is different for each major. Another way to state this is to say that choice of major is strongly related to sex, if the results are statistically significant. It is possible to represent the strength of this relationship with a coefficient of association such as the contingency coefficient or Phi. These coefficients are like the Pearson correlation and interpreted in roughly the same way.

Table 8-8b. Hypothetical Frequency Data		
	Psychology Majors	Biology Majors
Females	82	38
Males	21	59

The method for obtaining a chi-square test for independence is a little tricky. Begin by clicking **_Analyze_** → **_Descriptive Statistics_** → **_Crosstabs_**.... Transfer the variables to be analyzed to the **_Row(s)_** and **_Column(s)_** boxes. Then go to the **_Statistics..._** button and check the Chi-square box, **_Phi and Cramer's V_**, and anything else that looks interesting. Then click the **_Continue_** button. Next, click the **_Cells..._** button and check any needed descriptive information. *Percentages* are particularly useful for interpreting the data. Finally, click **_OK_** and the output will appear.

Sample results are shown in Tables 8-9a, 8-9b, and 8-9c. These data are part of a larger study used in development of a scale to measure lifelong learning. The two variables were Gender and In-class Texting. The In-class Texting question asked whether the person "regularly" sent text messages while they were in class. Table 8-8b shows the descriptive statistics (frequencies) for each variable.

Table 8-9a. Case Processing Summary

	Cases					
	Valid		Missing		Total	
	N	Percent	N	Percent	N	Percent
Gender * In-class Texting	471	98.1%	9	1.9%	480	100.0%

Table 8-9b. Gender * In-class Texting Crosstabulation

			Do you send text messages regularly during classes?		
			Yes	No	Total
Gender	Male	Count	23	168	191
		% within Gender	12.0%	88.0%	100.0%
		% within In-class Texting	36.5%	41.2%	40.6%
		% of Total	4.9%	35.7%	40.6%
	Female	Count	40	240	280
		% within Gender	14.3%	85.7%	100.0%
		% within IN-class Texting	63.5%	58.8%	59.4%
		% of Total	8.5%	51.0%	59.4%
Total		Count	63	408	471
		% within Gender	13.4%	86.6%	100.0%
		% within In-class Texting	100.0%	100.0%	100.0%
		% of Total	13.4%	86.6%	100.0%

The data in Table 8-9b were obtained by requesting all the available percentages in the cross-tabulation. The percentages help greatly in understanding the pattern of the results. In a research report, percentages across the variables will help the reader interpret the results.

Table 8-9c. Chi-Square Tests

	Value	df	Asymptotic Significance (2-sided)	Exact Sig. (2-sided)	Exact Sig. (1-sided)
Pearson Chi-Square	.493[a]	1	.482		
Continuity Correction[b]	.319	1	.572		
Likelihood Ratio	.498	1	.480		
Fisher's Exact Test				.582	.288
Linear-by-Linear Association	.492	1	.483		
N of Valid Cases	471				

a. 0 cells (0.0%) have expected count less than 5. The minimum expected count is 25.55.

b. Computed only for a 2x2 table

Table 8-9c shows the results of the chi-square analysis. The values for "Asymptotic Significance" are probabilities. A statistically significant result has a probability of less than .05. The first row "Pearson Chi-Square" shows the results for the typical chi-square analysis. The other outputs can be useful but are usually ignored. Following is an example of how to describe this result in a research article.

The relationship between biological sex and whether the individual reported regularly texting in class was not statistically significant, $\chi^2 (N = 471) = .493, p = .482$. It was found that 12.0% of males reported regularly texting in class versus 14.3% of females.

Analyzing Scales and Other Helpful Features of SPSS

There are several additional features available in SPSS that can be extremely helpful for any researcher. They will be described in this section.

Many researchers include a scale or measure in their research consisting of several items that are added to create a total score. Data analysis is performed on the total score for the items in the scale. SPSS makes it relatively easy to perform the necessary operations. For example, I have developed a scale called the Cell Phone Addiction Scale or CPAS and used it in several unpublished studies. The scale consists of 14 items with questions such as "I could not get along without my cell phone," and "I have tried unsuccessfully to cut back on using my cell phone." Each item is rated on a four-point scale ranging from *Completely false* (1 point) to *Completely true* (4 points). When used in research, the 14 scale items are labeled CPAS_01 through CPAS_14. Because it is a scale, the sum of the scores on the 14 items is obtained and data analysis is done on a variable called CPAS_Tot[al], which has a range of 14 to 56.

Transformations

Two particularly valuable features are available from the **_Transform_** menu: **_Recode_**, and **_Compute_**. The purpose of a recode is very simple. Imagine a variable that is coded from 1 to 5. Sometimes extreme values are not selected by very many individuals. Thus, it may be desirable to combine individuals who responded with either a 4 or a 5 into a single category such as 4. The recode feature is the way to do this. Another situation that often calls for a recode is when a variable is part of a scale, but the scoring needs to be reversed before it can be added to other items to make a total score. One of the steps in analyzing a measure or scale is to look at the item content or the scoring instructions provided by the author to determine whether any items are reversed scored. Reverse scoring is also accomplished with the recode command. Another scenario is that a variable might include a category such as "does not apply" which is coded as a "6." It would typically be more convenient to recode this value to "missing."

To do a recode, click **_Transform_** → **_Recode_** → **_Into Same Variables..._** or **_Into Different Variables..._** and enter the required information. The choice of recoding into the Same or Different Variables is a question of whether it is desirable to preserve the old data. By doing the recode into a Different variable, the old data can be preserved in case a mistake is made or another recoding procedure is tried. The Old and New Values option works for most situations. Figures 8-13 and 8-14 show how a variable can be reversed-scored.

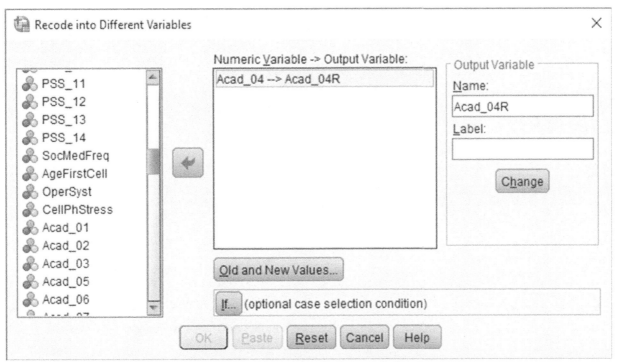

Figure 8-13. SPSS recode input dialog box.

The first input window to appear is shown in Figure 8-13, which allows the researcher to choose the variable to be recoded and give it a new name. The variable to be recoded is moved from the variable list on the left to the middle box. Type the new name in the "Output Variable" box. Then, click the **Change** button. This will add the new name to the center box. If several variables need to be re-coded in the same way, they can all be added at this time. The next step is to click the Old and New Values button, which results in the input window shown in Figure 8-14.

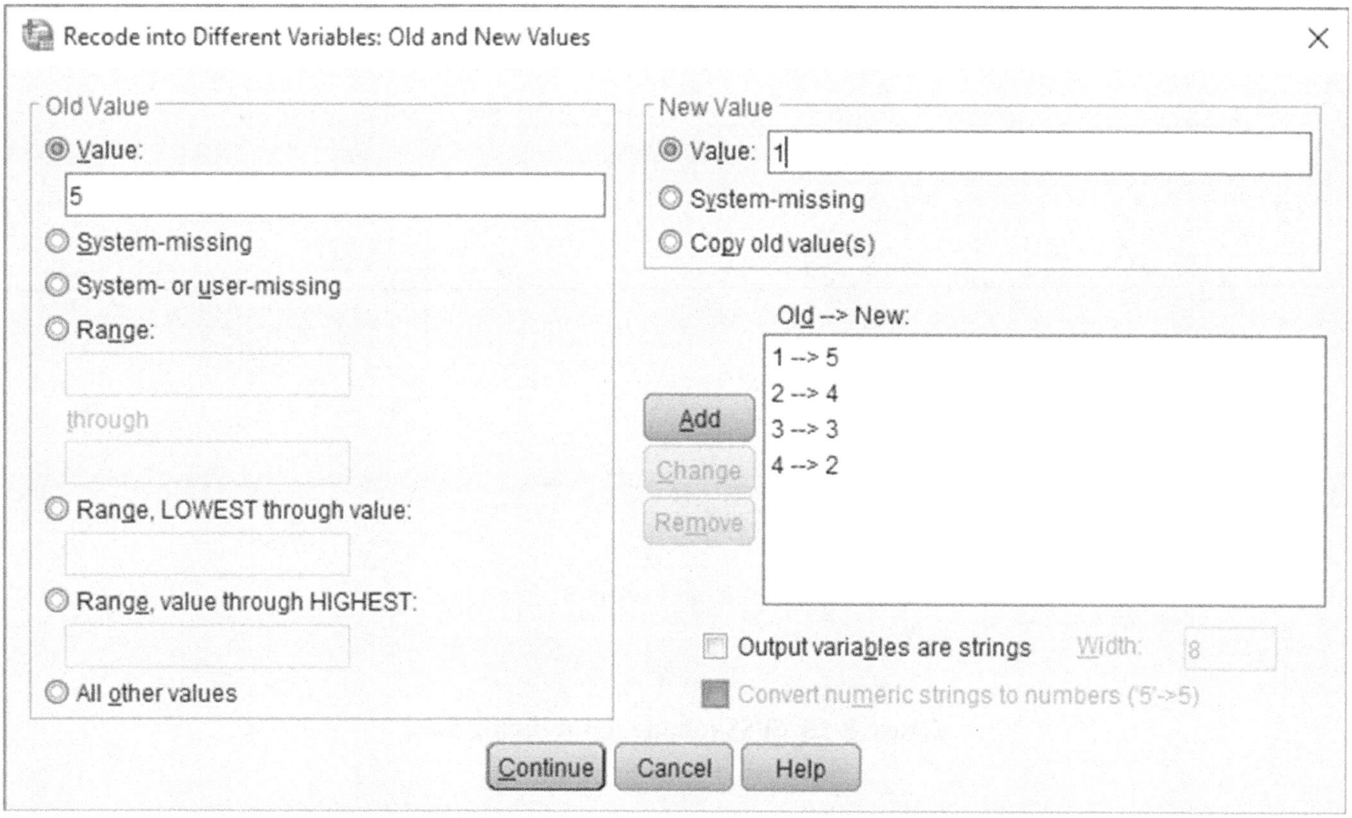

Figure 8-14. Old and New Values Input Window.

Using this window is simple. Enter the old values into the box on the left and the new values in the box on the right. After each pair of old and new values, click the **Add** button. The result this recode is that the variable will now be reversed-scored with high values becoming low values and low values becoming high values. Click **Continue** and **Okay**, and the recoded variable will appear at the end of the data file. Analyze the reverse-scored item like any other variable. The most likely use is adding the variable to other items to provide the total score of a scale or measure consisting of several items. Note that an old value can be changed to **System-missing** by clicking the appropriate button. This option is useful when it is necessary to eliminate an option such as "Does Not Apply."

The **Compute...** command is also under the **Transformations** menu. This command allows the researcher to construct an equation for changing the scale of a variable or adding items to create a total score. A transformation using the **Compute...** command can often bring data back into conformity with statistical assumptions. See Table 7-2 for a list of useful transformations. The **Compute...** option is also useful for computing the score of a measure. For example, if a dataset includes a scale that is scored by summing the answers to five questions, the **Compute...** option can be used to do this in seconds with 100% accuracy. To do this, go to **Transform → Compute Variable ....** Figure 8-15 shows the SPSS input window.

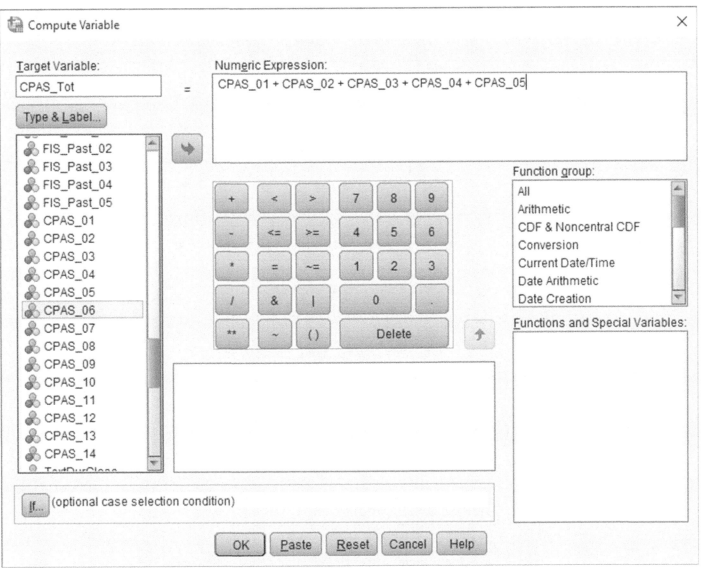

Figure 8-15. Input window for the SPSS compute command.

To use this input window, type a name for the new variable in the _**Target Variable**_ area. Then the scroll down the variable list which appears on the left. Use the arrow key to move variables to the "_**Numeric Expression**_" window. After moving each variable, hit the "**+**" key on the keypad. Continue with this sequence until all the necessary variables have been entered. Hitting the _**Okay**_ key on the bottom row of the window will cause the new variable to be computed. It will be added to the last column of the _**Data View**_ window. At this point the new variable (CPAS_Tot) can be used in any data analysis. However, for any report that might be created, it will also be necessary to compute coefficient alpha, an internal consistency measure of the reliability of the scale. See "Reliability Analysis" which appears below.

Before proceeding to reliability, there is one more compute function to review. As noted throughout this text, a useful way to address violations of assumptions is to perform a data transformation on the variable. One such transformation is to take the square root of the variable, which can often correct positive skew. Figure 8-16 illustrates how to do this. To execute this procedure, begin by typing the name of the new variable in the _**Target Variable:**_ box. Then go to the _**Function Group**_ box and select _**Arithmetic**_, which will cause the list of Functions and Special Variables to appear. Click _**Sqrt,**_ which will highlight it and then use the upward pointing arrow (to the immediate right of _**Delete**_) to move SQRT into the _**Numeric Expression:**_ box. **SQRT(?)** will appear in the _**Numeric Expression:**_ box. Then select the variable to be transformed (Col_GPA) and move it into the _**Numeric Expression:**_ box. The variable name will replace the question mark.

Clicking **OK** will execute the transformation and the new variable will be added to the end of the variable list. The transformed variable is then available to be included in any data analysis.

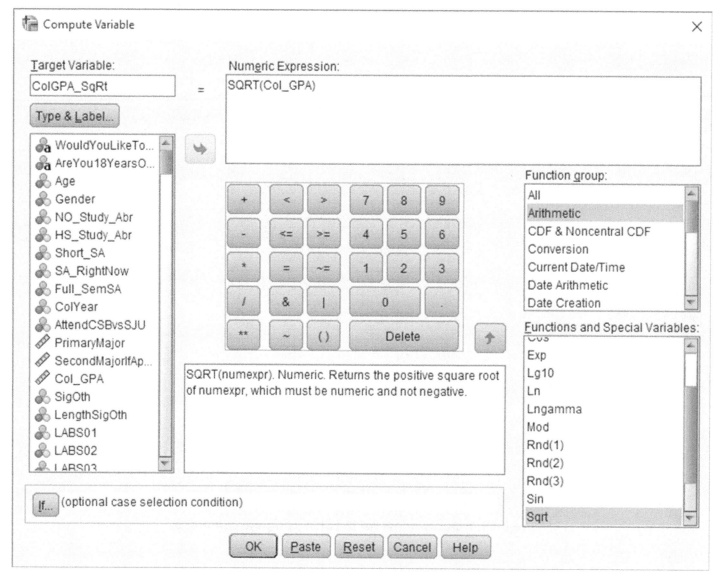

Figure 8-16. Square root transformation.

Reliability Analysis

Reliability is one of the most important characteristics of good measures. It is an estimate of the repeatability of a measure, that is, consistency over time. One way to compute reliability is to administer a test or measure once and then combine the correlations among all the items that make up the measure to create a measure of internal consistency called coefficient alpha or Cronbach's alpha. To compute the standard measure of internal consistency, coefficient alpha, click **_Analyze_ → _Scale_ → _Reliability Analysis_...**. The variables that make up the scale to be analyzed should be transferred to the **Items** box. Then click the **_Statistics..._** button and request all the descriptive statistics plus the item-total correlations. The item-total correlations provide important information about items that might be problematic such as those having unusually low correlations with the adjusted total score or negative correlations (Did you remember to use the reversed-scored alternative?). Research articles are expected to report reliabilities for all quantitative variables that are scored by summing individual items. The information provided in the output is valuable in the process of constructing new measures. This would be a focus of an advanced statistics class or a course in tests and measurements. A report of a survey study with numerous variables often includes a table with the names of variables, means, standard deviations, and coefficient alpha. Tables 8-10a and 8-10b show the output for reliability computations.

Table 8-10a. Reliability Statistics

Cronbach's Alpha	N of Items
.800	14

Table 8-10b. Item-Total Statistics for CPAS

	Scale Mean if Item Deleted	Scale Variance if Item Deleted	Corrected Item-Total Correlation	Cronbach's Alpha if Item Deleted
CPAS_01	32.11	35.126	.382	.733
CPAS_02	31.65	33.764	.421	.729
CPAS_03	31.15	34.266	.318	.741
CPAS_04	31.06	33.895	.580	.717
CPAS_05	31.95	32.734	.541	.715
CPAS_06	32.05	35.932	.260	.745
CPAS_07	32.60	34.575	.517	.723
CPAS_08	32.30	35.980	.294	.741
CPAS_09	32.53	36.986	.249	.745
CPAS_10	31.35	34.370	.521	.722
CPAS_11	31.90	33.959	.467	.724
CPAS_12	32.58	35.325	.413	.731
CPAS_13	32.25	34.427	.446	.727
CPAS_14	31.18	34.684	.396	.732
ACAD_04	30.79	42.385	-.278	.800

Table 8-10a reports a coefficient alpha for the CPAS of .800. This represents reliability for the CPAS after ACAD_04 was removed from the computations. The output in Table 8-10b shows the contribution that each individual item makes to the scale. The first two columns show the mean and variance of the scale if the item in the row is deleted. Under some circumstances, this information can be informative. The Corrected Item-Total Correlation shows the correlation of the score on the individual item with the total of the remaining items in the table. In other words, the first correlation of .382 is the correlation of CPAS_01 with the total of CPAS_02 through ACAD_04. Thus, the correlations in this column provide an indication of the performance of each individual item. Inspecting this column reveals a negative correlation of -.278 for the last item, ACAD_04. This item was inserted into the analysis to illustrate how a reliability analysis can reveal problems in the scale. A negative correlation could indicate that the item should have been reverse scored. A low correlation indicates a poorly performing item that could be removed from the scale. The last column in the table shows what will happen to the scale reliability if the item is removed. Generally, the information in these two columns can be used together to improve the performance of the scale and correct errors. Higher reliability is associated with more statistical power. Thus, researchers should begin with scales that maximize reliability, so they will be able to detect relationships and avoid Type II errors.

Exploratory Data Analysis

Exploratory data analysis is a process of carefully examining data prior to performing inferential statistical tests. Access to exploratory data analysis techniques can be obtained by clicking **_Statistics_** → **_Summarize_** → **_Explore..._** which leads to plots (boxplots; stem and leaf) and descriptive statistics that can help greatly in the early stages of data analysis. Distributions can also be tested for normality.

Help Features

The **_Help_** menu provides access to information about specific **_Topics_**, a **_Tutorial_**, a **_Statistics Coach_**, and other useful features. It is also possible to click the right mouse button while pointing to a term of interest which will result in a display of the definition of that term. The dialog or input boxes also have context-specific **_Help_** buttons.

Hierarchical Multiple Regression with SPSS

Multiple regression is an exceptionally versatile statistical technique. Researchers using survey techniques with large samples are particularly likely to find that multiple regression answers important questions about their data. Advanced statistics courses may spend an entire semester on multiple regression and related analytic tools. A concrete example will be used to illustrate the basic capabilities of multiple regression analyses.

The example is from an unpublished dataset. The purpose was to validate the Cell Phone Addiction Scale (CPAS) in the context of variables related to college student stress. The CPAS consists of 14 items with questions such as "I could not get along without my cell phone" "I have tried unsuccessfully to cut back on using my cell phone," "I am extremely anxious when I am without my cell phone," and "I use my cell phone when it is physically hazardous (e.g., while driving)." Each item is rated on a four-point scale ranging from *Completely false* (1 point) to *Completely true* (4 points). The study received IRB approval. I conducted a hierarchical multiple regression for which the dependent measure was the Perceived Stress Scale (PSS; Cohen, Kamarck, & Mermelstein, 1983). Three other variables were included in the analysis. The first was a four-item Extraversion scale published by Donnellan, Oswald, Baird, and Lucas (2006). The second measure asked students to rate themselves on three behaviors: "Get my homework done on time," "Do the reading required for class," and "Skip class deliberately, not due to illness" (reversed scored). Thus, this scale (called Academic) measured a student's tendency to perform basic behaviors needed for academic success. Fear of Intimacy (FIS; Descutner & Thelen, 1991) was also measured, based upon the hypothesis that lack of social relationships would be a significant source of stress for college students.

A hierarchical multiple regression begins with a hypothesis. The main purpose of the study was to validate the CPAS. The hypothesis was that students' preoccupation with their cell phones is a significant source of stress outweighing other factors. In other words, although each of the variables has statistically significant bivariate associations with stress, it was expected that these associations would not be statistically significant when the CPAS was entered first into a hierarchical regression. Controlling for cell phone addiction (i.e., entering CPAS first) should account for such a large proportion of stress that it leaves little for the remaining variables. A hierarchical multiple regression was used to determine the most important influences upon self-reported stress in college students, hypothesizing that the CPAS would be the most important predictor of stress among the variables included in the study. Four variables (CPAS, Extraversion, Fear of Intimacy, and the academic measure) were entered in the analysis. Figure 8-17 shows the main SPSS input screen for regression. To reach this input box go to **_Analyze_** → **_Regression_** → **_Linear_**.

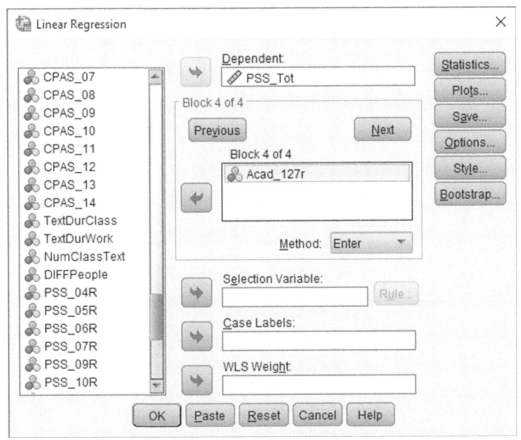

Figure 8-17. Input Screen for SPSS Multiple Regression

This input box allows the researcher to select the dependent variable and the independent variables in the order they will be entered in the regression analysis. Begin by selecting the dependent variable (the variable predicted by the other variables) and moving it into the **Dependent** box. Leave **Method** as **Enter** and ignore the **Selection Variable**, **Case Labels**, and **WLS Weight** boxes. After entering the first variable into the independent variable box (located below the **Dependent** box), click **Next** which will cause the second block to appear. Transfer the next independent variable into the box, click **Next**, and continue with this process until all the desired independent variables are entered. After all the variables have been transferred, click the **Statistics** button which will produce the box shown in Figure 8-18 and check the options that are relevant to your analysis. The boxes shown checked in Figure 8-18 will meet the needs of most researchers. The most important boxes are **Estimates**, **R squared change,** and **Part and partial correlations**. Click **Continue**, and then **OK** to execute the analysis.

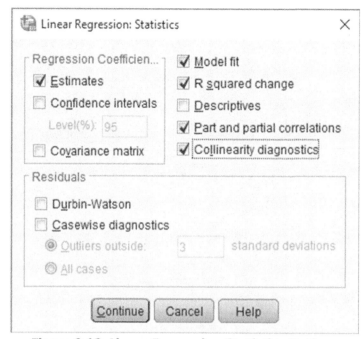

Figure 8-18. Linear Regression Statistics Options

Output Table 8-11a shows the variables that were entered and removed from the analysis. There is nothing interesting here because all the independent variables were included in the analysis because each made statistically significant contributions to predicting stress.

Table 8-11a. Variables Entered/Removed[a]

Model	Variables Entered	Variables Removed	Method
1	CPAS_Tot[b]	.	Enter
2	FIS[b]	.	Enter
3	Extraversion[b]	.	Enter
4	Academic[b]	.	Enter

a. Dependent Variable: PSS_Tot

b. All requested variables entered.

Output Table 8-11b shows how much each successive step or block contributed to predicting the dependent variable over and above the previous block(s).

Table 8-11b. Model Summary

Model	R	R Square	Adjusted R Square	Std. Error of the Estimate	Change Statistics: R Square Change	F Change	df1	df2	Sig. F Change
1	.262[a]	.068	.066	6.75139	.068	26.281	1	358	.000
2	.342[b]	.117	.112	6.58245	.049	19.611	1	357	.000
3	.369[c]	.136	.129	6.51817	.020	8.076	1	356	.005
4	.451[d]	.203	.194	6.27098	.066	29.620	1	355	.000

a. Predictors: (Constant), CPAS

b. Predictors: (Constant), CPAS, FIS

c. Predictors: (Constant), CPAS, FIS, Extraversion

d. Predictors: (Constant), CPAS, FIS, Extraversion, Academic

The footnotes indicate the variables included in each model. ***R*** and ***R Square*** are the multiple correlation and squared multiple correlation coefficients. Their interpretation is similar to the bivariate correlation coefficient except that the multiple correlation represents the strength of the linear relationship between the dependent variable and the non-overlapping portions of the independent variables. The ***Std. Error of the Estimate*** is prediction error from using the independent variables to predict the dependent variable. ***R Square Change*** shows the incremental change in ***R Square*** for each model compared to the previous model. Finally, ***Change Statistics*** show whether the incremental change in R Square was statistically significant. As each variable was added to the regression, it made an additional and statistically significant contribution to predicting stress. For example, ***Model 3*** adds Extraversion to the variables in ***Model 2***. The results show that Extraversion made a significant contribution to predicting Stress, $F(1, 356) = 8.076$, $p = .005$, above the contribution made by the CPAS and Fear of Intimacy (FIS) in ***Model 2***. Thus, the hypothesis that the CPAS would outweigh the other variables was not supported. The ***ANOVA*** table (not shown) is self-explanatory and indicates the overall statistical significance for each model.

Table 8-11c, ***Coefficients***, shows the overall picture of the relative contribution of each variable to predicting stress. The regression coefficients, *t*-values, and their statistical significance can be reported in the results. For each model, the output shows the **Zero-order** correlation, which is the bivariate correlation between each predictor variable and the dependent variable. The ***Partial*** correlation between the CPAS and stress (PSS) of .204 shows the amount of relationship that remains between stress and the CPAS when the other three variables are controlled or partialed out of both the independent and dependent variables. The ***Part*** correlation is the *Semipartial* correlation, a term used in most statistics books where one can find a lot of discussion of differences between Part and Semipartial correlations. The Semipartial correlations provide a measure of the additional variation predicted by each independent variable when all other variables have been accounted for. The *t*-test for ***(Constant)*** indicates whether the constant in the regression equation differs significantly from zero. This information is interesting only when the variables have been standardized (converted to *z*-scores).

The results in ***Model 4*** indicate that the CPAS contributes significantly to predicting stress, independently of the remaining variables in the analysis, with a Part Correlation of .186. However, the results also show a substantial and statistically significant correlation between stress and academic behavior even after controlling for cell phone addiction, fear of intimacy, and extraversion. Less stress was associated with more frequently engaging in productive academic behavior. This was unexpected because it was predicted that cell phone addiction would interfere with intimate relationships and academic behaviors. It was also predicted that Extraversion would be a buffer against stress, which was supported by the zero-order correlation of -.167, but it was not expected that this relationship would remain strong after controlling for the other variables in the analysis, especially cell phone addiction. Thus, the conclusion is that cell phone addiction is one of several variables associated with stress in college students. Cell phone addiction does not have a dominant role as predicted.

The last two columns of Table 8-11c, **Tolerance** and **VIF** (variance inflation factor) are both indicators of multicolinearity, which distorts the results of multiple regression. Values for **Tolerance** should be above .10 and values for **VIF** should be below 10. In all cases, the values in Table 8-10c are acceptable.

Table 8-11c. Coefficients[a]

Model		Unstandardized Coefficients		Standardized Coefficients			Correlations			Collinearity Statistics	
		B	Std. Error	Beta	t	Sig.	Zero-order	Partial	Part	Tolerance	VIF
1	(Constant)	31.839	1.727		18.435	.000					
	CPAS	.280	.055	.262	5.127	.000	.262	.262	.262	1.000	1.000
2	(Constant)	28.962	1.805		16.046	.000					
	CPAS	.240	.054	.224	4.436	.000	.262	.229	.221	.972	1.029
	FIS	.350	.079	.223	4.428	.000	.261	.228	.220	.972	1.029
3	(Constant)	32.212	2.122		15.181	.000					
	CPAS	.251	.054	.234	4.680	.000	.262	.241	.230	.966	1.035
	FIS	.309	.080	.197	3.871	.000	.261	.201	.191	.938	1.066
	Extraversion	-.254	.089	-.143	-2.842	.005	-.167	-.149	-.140	.964	1.037
4	(Constant)	48.552	3.631		13.373	.000					
	CPAS	.205	.052	.192	3.921	.000	.262	.204	.186	.941	1.063
	FIS	.237	.078	.151	3.045	.002	.261	.160	.144	.912	1.097
	Extraversion	-.278	.086	-.156	-3.234	.001	-.167	-.169	-.153	.962	1.040
	Academic	-1.061	.195	-.267	-5.442	.000	-.328	-.278	-.258	.935	1.069

a. Dependent Variable: PSS

Reporting Hierarchical Multiple Regression Results

Reporting multiple regression results can be tremendously complicated depending upon the hypotheses and analytic approach. The following illustrates one approach to describing these results. Browsing various professional journals will lead to many other approaches and models of how to perform and report analyses.

A hierarchical multiple regression was conducted to investigate the relationship of stress and cell phone addiction. I hypothesized that CPAS scores would be the most important predictor of stress among the variables included in the study. Four variables (CPAS score, Fear of Intimacy, Extraversion, & Academic Behavior) were entered into the analysis and all variables made significant contributions to predicting stress. Table 1 [8-10d] summarizes the results. Contrary to the hypothesis, the CPAS was about equal to the other measures in their ability to predict college student stress. It was expected that controlling for cell phone addiction with the CPAS would eliminate or decrease the contribution of the other variables, because cell phone use has the potential to interfere with study habits, social interaction, and forming intimate relationships. In contrast, all four variables made statistically significant contributions to predicting stress in college students.

TABLE 1 [8-11d]

Multiple Regression of College Stress (PSS)

	B	β	Part r	t	Significance
CPAS	.205	.192	.186	3.92	.000
FIS	.237	.151	.144	3.05	.002
Extraversion	-.278	-.156	-.153	-3.23	.001
Academic	-1.061	-.267	-.258	-5.44	.000

$R^2 = .203$
Adjusted $R^2 = .194$
$R = .451$, $p = .000$

Note. $N = 360$

Conclusion

This chapter described some basic analyses and points the way toward more advanced procedures. As you gain skills, you will become capable of performing very complex analyses. The best way to learn the advanced features of SPSS is to explore the program using data from an original study, learning by trial-and-error, and then doing additional research on the issues that are problematic. Keep in mind that SPSS is much faster, convenient, and accurate than computing an analysis by hand. Allow enough time for studying statistics textbooks, exploring options, and interpreting the output at each stage. Although computation of one correlation coefficient takes a few seconds, analysis of an entire study may take weeks or longer. Every data analysis should begin with the "Frequencies" procedure for each variable, which allows easy identification of outliers and out-of-range data (e.g., a value that is beyond what is allowable). The Frequencies output also allows identification of imbalances in the sample such as too few males or too many first-year students. Then, use histograms to examine key variables for normality. After examining the frequency distributions, return to the original questions that inspired the research to develop your ideas about appropriate analyses. Howell (2010), Mertler and Vannatta (2013), or Tabachnick and Fidell (2013) are excellent resources for researchers who wish to learn more about advanced statistical procedures.

Review Questions and Exercises for Chapter 8

1. When you have difficulties with SPSS, it is important to persist until you solve the problem, even if it takes dozens of hours. TRUE or FALSE

2. Use the same data shown in Table 8-1 and compute the correlation using SPSS.

3. The following table contains various probabilities (Sig.) from SPSS output. If the probability would be associated with a statistically significant result, write "Yes" in the second column. If the probability would NOT be a statistically significant result write "NS" in the second column.

Sig.	Interpretation
.060	
.100	
.500	
.005	
.000	
.200	
.800	
1.00	
.001	
.070	
.030	
.020	

4. If a dataset contains a nominal (categorical) variable with two categories, you might see that variable included in a correlation matrix.   TRUE   FALSE

5. Describe the characteristics of each of the two variables needed to perform an independent groups t-test.

6. If Levene's Test for Equality of Variances is statistically significant, what does it mean?

7. What is the input required for a dependent or paired samples t-test.

8. What is the basic rule indicating an analysis of variance is appropriate?

9. What characterizes a factorial ANOVA?

10. How many F-ratios need to be interpreted in a 2 X 2 Factorial design?

11. What does a statistically significant chi-square test of independence indicate?

12. What procedure would be used to change a value of "6" to "missing" for a particular variable in a study?

13. What is coefficient alpha? What does it mean?

14. What is the most likely cause of a strong negative correlation in the corrected item-total correlations for a reliability analysis?

15. What is the value of the **_Compute..._** option?

16. What is the meaning of a **_Partial_** correlation?

Answers to Chapter 8 Review

1. FALSE. If you experience difficulty call or visit your institution's Helpdesk, search for information on your local network, contact your instructor, or ask for help from your peers.

2. Your output should precisely match the output shown below.

Descriptive Statistics

	Mean	Std. Deviation	N
ColGPA	2.9455	.72851	11
StudyHrs	23.8182	13.40014	11

Correlations

		ColGPA	StudyHrs
ColGPA	Pearson Correlation	1	.868**
	Sig. (2-tailed)		.001
	N	11	11
StudyHrs	Pearson Correlation	.868**	1
	Sig. (2-tailed)	.001	
	N	11	11

**. Correlation is significant at the 0.01 level (2-tailed).

3. See the table below for correct answers.

Sig.	Interpretation
.060	NS
.100	NS
.500	NS
.005	Significant
.000	Significant
.200	NS
.800	NS
1.00	NS
.001	Significant
.070	NS
.030	Significant
.020	Significant

4. TRUE. The main application of the correlation coefficient is to determine the strength of the linear relationship between two quantitative variables. The information contained in the correlation is the same as would be provided by conducting an independent groups t-test. If you are taking an introductory statistics course, the rule that correlation can be used only for two quantitative measures typically cannot be broken.

5. The two variables need to perform an independent groups t-test are:
   a. Independent variable: A grouping variable, nominal level of measurement; measured or manipulated; the variable must have two categories or levels.
   b. Dependent variable: a quantitative measured variable.

6. The assumption of homogeneous variances (that the two populations have the same variance) has been violated.

7. The same variable needs to be measured at two different times.
8. The researcher is interested in differences among more than two means of a quantitative dependent variable.
9. There is more than one independent (grouping) variable.
10. Three; the two main effects plus the interaction.
11. The two variable are dependent or related to each other.
12. Use the → **Recode** → **Into Same Variables...** or **Into Different Variables...** command which is found under the **Transform** menu.
13. Coefficient alpha is an internal consistency estimate of reliability. It is an estimate of the repeatability of a measure calculated by combining the information in the correlations of the items in the scale with each other.
14. An item that was supposed to be reverse-scored remains in the scale in its unreversed format.
15. The **Compute...** option can be used to do a data transformation or to compute the total score of a variable that consists of the sum of scores on several items.
16. A partial correlation correlates the independent variable and the dependent variable after the linear effects of other variables have been removed from *both* the independent variable and the dependent variable.

Glossary

Bayes Theorem: This is an alternative or supplement to NHST, the heart of which is a formula for calculating the probability of an event given the previous or prior probability and the addition of new information. For example, given a base rate of a disease such as infectious mononucleosis of 5%, how much would the probability of having the disease change by knowing that one has a positive outcome of a test for mono? This problem is more complex than it might seem because both the probability of having the disease and the probability of a false positive must be included in the computations. Furthermore, a low or moderate rate of false positives can result in a surprisingly low probability of actually having the disease, given a positive test result. In hypothesis testing, estimation of the prior probability can be problematic because belief in a theory or empirical finding can be difficult to state precisely. In short, Bayes Theorem is a formal way of calculating how past beliefs are changed by new information. In applying Bayes Theorem to research, it is necessary to guess or estimate some probabilities that enter into Bayes equation. See Howell (2010) for a more detailed discussion of Bayes Theorem and how it is applied.

Beyond: The word *beyond* is a deliberate word choice in two-tailed tests of significance. In this context, it means "away from the mean." For example, if a test of significance was being conducted with z-scores and the cutoffs were +1.96 or -1.96, a statistically significant result would be indicated by a *z*-score above +1.96 or below -1.96. Another way to say this is that the obtained value must be beyond the cutoffs.

Bimodal distribution: A frequency distribution that has two peaks or modes. If the modes are a good distance apart with lower frequencies in between, further investigation would be needed. The variable might need to be excluded from some analyses or transformed because it violates the assumption of normality.

Bootstrapping: Bootstrapping is a statistical technique that creates a distribution of means, variances, *SD*s, correlations, or another sample statistic from an original dataset. The technique begins with the original sample data. Then, a thousand or more samples of the original data are taken with replacement. "With replacement" means that after each value is taken from the sample and recorded, it is replaced in the sample. This means that each complete sample can contain duplicates of values from the original data. By taking thousands of such samples from the original dataset, a distribution can be created that accurately shows the variability of the sample statistic. This information can be used to construct accurate confidence intervals that do not require meeting the assumptions of parametric statistics. Bootstrapping is becoming a more popular technique as computing power becomes so available and cheap.

Causal claim: A causal claim is a claim that changes in one variable cause changes in another variable. Three conditions are associated with a valid causal claim (e.g., Morling, 2018):
- Covariance: Changes in one of the variables are associated with changes in the other variable.
- Temporal precedence: The causal variable (A) precedes or comes before the other variable (B). That is, causes come before effects.
- Internal validity: Alternative explanations for the change in B are ruled out by the design of the study. In other words, the causal variable is the only thing that changed in the study.

Central Limit Theorem: The Central Limit Theorem is a mathematical proof that a variable consisting of the sum of a large number of independent variables will distribute as a normal distribution. Furthermore, regardless of the shape of the original distribution, the distribution of means will tend toward a normal distribution as the sample size increases. The Central Limit Theorem is one of the foundations of inferential statistics.

Coefficient alpha: A way to compute reliability of a measure. The measures is administered once and the correlations among all the items that make up the measure are combined to create a measure of internal consistency called coefficient alpha or Cronbach's alpha. Coefficient alpha is easier to compute than test-retest reliability because it requires that the test be administered only once. Consequently, research articles are somewhat more likely to report coefficient alpha than test-retest reliability. Reliability is reported as a number between 0.0 and 1.00.

Confidence interval: A confidence interval is a range of values within which the true population value will lie. For example, if a child obtained a score of 120 on an IQ test, a confidence interval around that value would specify a range of values within which the child's "true" score would be. One way to conceptualize the true score is that it represents the average of scores that would be obtained if the test could be administered to the same child many times. Use of confidence intervals has been proposed as an alternative to Null Hypothesis Significance Testing (NHST). This technique takes the same information available from a typical statistical test and uses it to construct confidence intervals around the obtained value of the test statistic. If the interval contains zero (in the case of an independent means *t*-test), the result is not significant. A major advantage of using confidence intervals is that researchers remain aware of the variability associated with their results.

Data transformation: Data transformations are used to correct non-normal distributions or heterogeneous variances. To do a data transformation, each individual score is subjected to an arithmetic operation, such as taking the square root of each value. A square root transformation has a bigger impact on larger numbers so it can potentially correct positive skew. Other useful data transformations include reciprocal, log, and arcsine.

Degrees of freedom: The number of scores that are "free to vary" in a statistical calculation. For example, given a fixed value for the mean, all of the scores except one are free to vary because the last value is restricted to a certain value in order to have the mean of the numbers equal to the fixed value. For many statistical calculations, the number of degrees of freedom is $N - 1$. Degrees of freedom are part of the SPSS output and are usually reported along with the test statistic.

Dependent variable: A dependent variable is defined as "the 'outcome' variable that is observed to occur or change after the occurrence or variation of the independent variable. Dependent variables may or may not be related causally to the independent variable" (American Psychological Association, 2007, p. 269).

Descriptive statistics: The process of describing a group of numbers. Common descriptive statistics are measures of central tendency (mode, median, and mean) and measures of spread or dispersion (range, standard deviation, and variance).

False negative: When the result of a diagnostic procedure or test is negative, but the test should have indicated a positive result. In NHST logic a Type II error could be considered a false negative.

False positive: When the result of a diagnostic procedure or test is positive but the test should have indicated a negative result. In NHST logic, a Type I error could be considered a false positive.

Figure: A figure in APA style contains a graphic representation of numbers, such as a histogram or scatterplot, whereas a table contains numbers and text only. Tables and figures are numbered separately in APA style writing and in *QRST*.

General linear Model: An overarching model that is used to model statistical analysis in the general case, independent of the particular statistical method. The model consists of a dependent variable, which is equal to a linear combination of weighted predictor variables plus error or unaccounted for variance.

Grouping variable: A nominal variable that is used to place participants into groups. By convention a grouping variable is also called an independent variable.

Independent variable: The *APA Dictionary of Psychology* (American Psychological Association, 2007) defines an independent variable as "the variable in an experiment that is specifically manipulated or is observed to occur before the occurrence of the dependent, or outcome, variable. Independent variables may or may not be causally related to the dependent variable. In statistical analysis, an independent variable is likely to be referred to as a predictor variable" (p. 475).

Inferential statistics: The process of making inferences about a population from the information in a sample.

Manipulated variable: A variable that is controlled by a researcher so that the researcher is capable of assigning any subject to experience any level of the variable. Random assignment of subjects to groups is a requirement for having a manipulated variable. The presence of a manipulated variable supports a causal claim.

Mean: The average of a group of numbers. It is found by adding up all the scores for a variable and dividing by the number of scores.

Measured variable: The values of a variable that are measured or recorded by the researcher. Alternately, a measured variable may by reported by the participants in a study.

Median: The middle score in a distribution. The median divides the distribution in half, with half of the frequency count above the median and half below the median. The median lies at the 50th percentile of any distribution.

Mode: The value of a variable with the highest frequency count.

Negative skew: Negative skew means that the variable has some extreme values at the lower end. In looking at a histogram, the narrow or pointed part of the histogram will point toward the negative end of the number line. Negative skew tends to draw the mean toward the skew so that the mean is a lower value than the median.

Nonparametric statistical tests: Nonparametric tests do not make any assumptions about the populations. Table 7-1 shows a few common nonparametric tests. See Siegel (1956) for a more complete list.

Normal distribution: A normal distribution has a defined set of mathematical characteristics defined by a complex mathematical equation. A normal curve is a frequency distribution that is bell-shaped and symmetrical. The mode, median, and mean are all equal in a normal curve. Figure 1-4 shows several examples of normal curves. Many inferential statistics assume that the population distribution for quantitative variables in the analysis are normally distributed. However, the Central Limit Theorem guarantees that most distributions will be close to normally distributed, given an adequate sample size.

Orthogonal: In a graph of variables such as a factor analysis, the axes are at right angles to each other. Another way to say this is that they are independent or uncorrelated. The variables in a factorial ANOVA are not orthogonal when there are unequal numbers of subjects in the cells of the design. This creates interesting issues in the interpretation of the interactions and marginal means.

Outliers: Outliers are values on a variable that lie beyond a reasonable range for that variable. One way to identify outliers is to create a boxplot for the variable. When outliers are discovered, the researcher needs to make a decision regarding how to deal with them.

Parametric statistical tests: Parametric tests make critical assumptions about the data. For example, most parametric tests assume the population distribution is normal and population variances of groups are homogeneous. The *t*-tests, ANOVA, correlation, and multiple regression are the most frequently used parametric tests.

Parsimony: Parsimony is a scientific principle that states the simplest theoretical explanation of a phenomenon should be favored over a more complex theory, other things being equal. Other terms for this principle are Occam's razor and Morgan's Cannon.

Part correlation: A component of SPSS multiple regression output. The *Part* correlation is called the semipartial correlation in most statistics books. It provides a measure of the additional variation predicted by an independent variable added to a regression equation after the linear effects of the other variables have been removed from the independent variable and but not the dependent variable. Thus, the "semi" of semipartial reveals the meaning of the term because second IV is partialed from the first IV but not the DV. This results in a measure of the unique contribution of the first IV to predicting the DV.

Partial correlation: A partial correlation correlates the independent variable and the dependent variable after the linear effects of other variables have been removed from *both* the independent variable and the dependent variable. Thus, subtraction of the effects of other variables applies to both the independent and dependent variables and the partial correlation provides a measure of the relationship between the IV and DV controlling for the relationship of a third variable to both the IV and DV. Another way to say this is that the partial correlation represents the correlation between the IV and DV when a third variable has been statistically controlled or held constant.

Percentile rank: A percentile rank indicates the percent of scores that lie at or below a particular value of a variable. For example, the score that lies at the 20th percentile has 20% of the scores in the distribution at or below it.

Population: The population is the entire group of scores or people to which a researcher intends that the results will apply.

Positive skew: Positive skew means that a distribution of scores has extreme values at the upper end. The narrow, pointed, or skewed end of the distribution points in the positive direction on the number line. A distribution with positive skew has a mean that is higher than the median.

Quantitative: In *QRST*, this term defines a variable for which the numerical values indicate an amount or quantity of a characteristic. Therefore, it would make sense to compute a mean or average value for the variable. Such variables could also be correlated with each other or included in a multiple regression analysis assuming they are close to normally distributed.

Random assignment: This is a method of assigning subject to conditions in which each subject has an equal probability of being assigned to any condition. Random assignment to the levels of a variable indicates that the variable is manipulated.

Random sample: A random sample consists of a portion of a population in which each member of the population has an equal chance of being selected for the sample. Placing all the names of members of a population into a hat and drawing names randomly from the hat would be one way to obtain a random sample of a population. In practice, true random samples of a population are difficult to obtain because subjects can refuse to participate and it is difficult to obtain complete lists of target populations.

Regression to the mean: Regression to the mean is a statistical phenomenon in which predicted values get closer to the mean when the correlation is less than 1.00. The more extreme the value being predicted from is (i.e., the further away from the mean in either direction), the more pronounced regression to the mean will be. In research design, regression to the mean can look like change brought about by an experimental manipulation if the research begins with a group with extreme scores at the beginning of the study.

Reliability: The basic definition of reliability is the repeatability of a test or measure. In other words, would the test provide the same score if it was administered twice? A frequently used analogy is a bathroom scale. If a person weighed themselves twice, with ten minutes between measurements, they would expect their weight to be the same on both occasions because weight does not change much over such a brief time period. The two ways of assessing reliability of a measure are test-retest and internal consistency (coefficient alpha).

Repeated measure: A repeated measure design measures each person in a study at different points in time. These designs are very powerful because each subject serves as their own control, which greatly reduces random variation. An example of a repeated measure design would be a study in which each person is tested in a driving